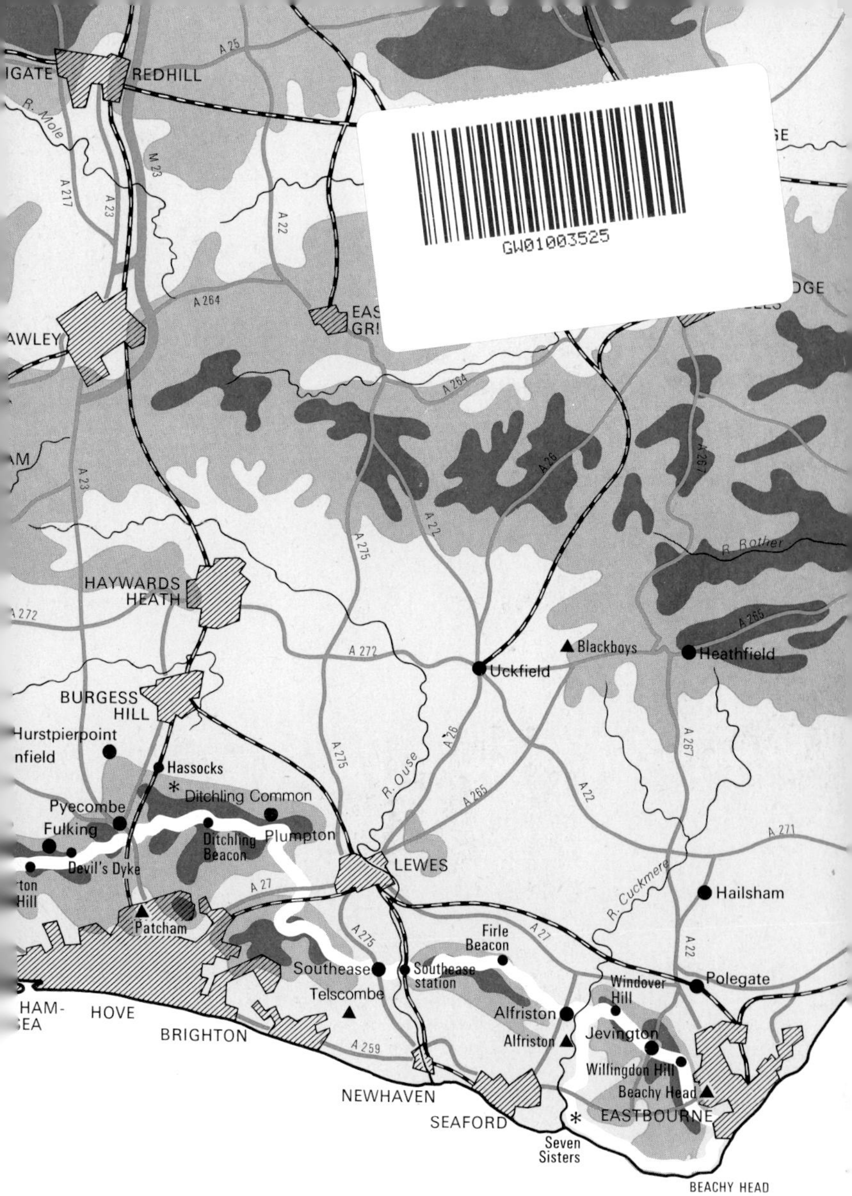

Roads

Railways

Youth hostels

Country Parks

0 10 Miles

0 15 Kilometres

South Downs Way

To Derek,
Happy Walking!
(with me!)
Christmas 1987,
Micheline

Seán Jennett

Long Distance Path Guide No 7

Revised edition

London Her Majesty's Stationery Office
Published for the Countryside Commission

Front and back covers
View west from Ditchling Beacon
Frontispiece
Aerial view of downs at Fulking *(Aerofilms)*
Endpaper
Long Man of Wilmington

The maps in this guide are extracts from Ordnance Survey maps 1:25,000 or about 2½ inches to 1 mile, and have been prepared from O.S. Sheets SU 71, 81, 91; TQ 01, 00, 10, 11, 20, 30, 21, 31, 40, 50; TV 49, 59, 69.

Drawings
Harry Titcombe: Cover, pp 17, 20, 21, 22, 26, 29, 33, 36, 46, 54, 58, 66, 72, 78, 79, 83, 88, 98
John Western: pp 10–11, 39, 46, 59, 73

First published 1977
Second impression 1983

Government Bookshops
49 High Holborn, London WC1V 6HB
13a Castle Street, Edinburgh EH2 3AR
Brazennose Street, Manchester M60 8AS
Southey House, Wine Street, Bristol BS1 2BQ
258 Broad Street, Birmingham B1 2HE
80 Chichester Street, Belfast BT1 4JY
Government publications are also available through booksellers

The waymark sign is used in plaque and stencil form by the Countryside Commission on long-distance footpaths

Other Long Distance Path Guides published for the Countryside Commission by HMSO:
The Pennine Way, by Tom Stephenson: 120 pages, £3.95 net
The Cleveland Way, by Alan Falconer: 144 pages, £3.95 net
The Pembrokeshire Coast Path, by John H. Barratt: 124 pages, £3.95 net
Offa's Dyke Path, by John B. Jones: 124 pages, £3.95 net
Cornwall Coast Path, by Edward C. Pyatt: 124 pages, £3.95 net
The Ridgeway Path, by Seán Jennett: 124 pages, £3.95 net
Dorset Coast Path, by Brian Jackman: 122 pages, £3.95 net
South Devon Coast Path, by Brian Le Messurier: 122 pages, £3.95 net
Somerset and North Devon Coast Path, by Clive Gunnell: 112 pages, £3.95 net
The North Downs Way, by Denis Herbstein: 148 pages, £3.95 net
The Wolds Way, by Roger Ratcliffe: 128 pages, £3.95 net

Countryside Commission
John Dower House
Crescent Place
Cheltenham, Glos. GL50 3RA

Prepared for the Countryside Commission by the Central Office of information 1977 revised edition 1983
Printed in the UK for HMSO

ISBN 0 11 700840 0 Dd 696423 C250 4/83 Pro 17492

Contents

Maps of route

Acknowledgements
Acknowledgements for assistance in writing this book are due to: Mr Charles Shippam, Blue Circle Cement Co. Ltd., the Youth Hostels Association, the East and West Sussex County Councils, the Hampshire County Council, the Forestry Commission, the Society of Sussex Downsmen, the Butser Ancient Farm Project.

Maps reference

SOUTH DOWNS WAY

Entry and exit points for riders

Note:- Road fillings and numbers are shown in orange on the map.

Motorway, Trunk and Main Road (Dual Carriageway)	M 4 *or* A 6(M)	A 123 *or* A 123(T)
Trunk & Main Road	A 123 *or*	A 123(T)
Secondary Road	*Fenced* B 2314	*Unfenced*
Road Under Construction		
Other Roads	*Good, metalled*	*Poor, or unmetalled*
Footpaths	*FP* *Fenced*	*FP* *Unfenced*
Railways, Multiple Track	Station, *Sidings*, *Road over*, *Cutting*	*Tunnel*, *FB* *(Footbridge)*
,, *Single Track*	*Viaduct*, *Level Crossing*	*Embankment*, *Road under*
,, *Narrow Gauge*		
Aerial Ropeway	*Aerial Ropeway*	
Boundaries *County or County Borough*		
,, ,, ,, ,, ,, ,, *with Parish*		
,, *Parish*		
Pipe Line (Oil, Water)	*Pipe Line*	

Electricity Transmission Lines (Pylons shown at bends and spaced conventionally)

Post Offices (In Villages & Rural Areas only) P — *Town Hall* TH — *Public House* PH

Church or Chapel with Tower — *Church or Chapel with Spire* — *Church or Chapel without either*

Triangulation Station △ — *on Church with Tower* — *without Tower*

Intersected Point on Chy ⊙ — *on Church with Spire* — *without Spire* — *on Building*

Guide Post *GP.* — *Mile Post* *MP.* — *Mile Stone* *MS.* — *Boundary Stone* *BS* ∘ — *Boundary Post* *BP* ∘

Youth Hostel Y — *Telephone Call Box (Public)* T — *(AA)* A — *(RAC)* R — *Antiquity (site of)*

Public Buildings	*Glasshouses*
Quarry & Gravel Pit	*Orchard*
National Trust Area (*Sheen Common NT*)	*Furze*
Osier Bed	*Rough Pasture Heath & Moor*
Reeds	*Marsh*
Park, Fenced	*Well* W ∘
	Spring Spr ∘
Wood, Coniferous, Fenced	*Wind Pump* *Wd Pp.*
Wood, Non-Coniferous Unfenced	*Contours are at 25 feet vertical interval.*
Brushwood, Fenced & Unfenced	*Spot Height* 123·

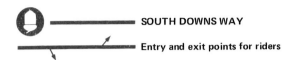

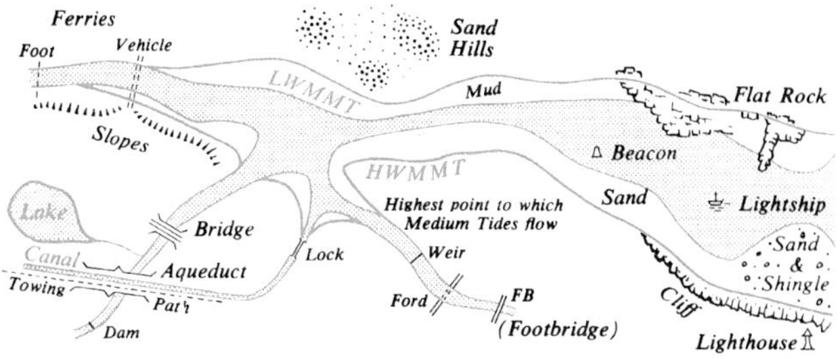

Note:- Sand is shown as an orange stipple on the map. Sand and shingle are shown in orange, and mud as a combined blue and orange stipple.

The symbols shown below appear only on second series OS maps which are used on maps 4, 5, 6, 7, 8 and 9 and part of maps 3 and 10

PUBLIC RIGHTS OF WAY

Public paths: Footpath; Bridleway

Road used as a public path

The representation on this map of any other road, track or path is no evidence of the existence of a right of way

SYMBOLS

▲ Youth hostel

NT National Trust always open

NT National Trust opening restricted

VEGETATION

Coniferous trees

Non-coniferous trees

Coppice

Orchard

HEIGHTS AND ROCK FEATURES

50 · ground survey; 285 · air survey — Determined by

Surface heights are to the nearest metre above mean sea level. Heights shown close to a triangulation pillar refer to the station height at ground level and not necessarily to the summit

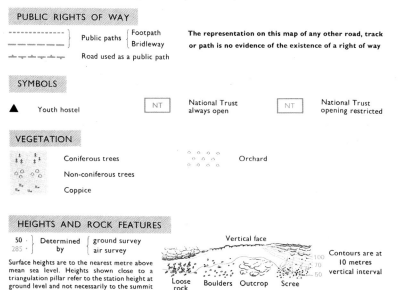

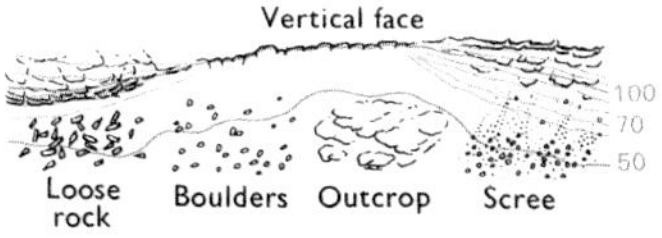

Contours are at 10 metres vertical interval

It should be noted that the footpath section from Eastbourne to Alfriston, along the cliff-tops by way of Beachy Head and the Seven Sisters and up to the Cuckmere Valley, is neither suitable nor accessible for horses or for cyclists. It is for walkers only.

The maps in this guide show the South Downs Way adequately on a scale of 1:25,000 (about 2½ inches to the mile). A large spread on the same scale is shown by the Ordnance Survey's Outdoor Leisure Map of Brighton and Sussex Vale, which covers the Way from a point south of Kingston near Lewes westwards to a point near Upper Beeding; on this map the Way is indicated by a thick, green, pecked line.

The 1:25,000 maps may not extend sufficiently far to allow identification of places seen in the wide panoramas for which the South Downs Way is notable. The Ordnance Survey 1:50,000 map (about 1¼ inches to the mile), includes more country north and south of the Way. The sheets required are, from east to west: 199, 198, and 197. The last of these does not quite include Old Winchester Hill, which will be found on sheet 185, which also includes Winchester itself.

SOUTH DOWNS WAY
SOUTH DOWNS WAY
SOUTH DOWNS WAY
DUNCTON
TEGLEAZE
JWP
CS
JBS
FN
LEE FARM
AMBERLEY
SOUTH DOWNS WAY
SOUTH
DOWNS WAY
CLAYTON MILLS
BEACON
KEYMER POST

Bridleway and footpath

The South Downs Way was one of six long-distance paths recommended in 1947 by the Special Committee on Footpaths and Access to the Countryside set up under the chairmanship of Sir Arthur Hobhouse. The original intention was that the route should run from Eastbourne to Winchester, where it would join the Pilgrims' Way and continue to a point west of Salisbury. The full distance of this intention was not realised. The National Parks Commission (the predecessor of the Countryside Commission) submitted a report to the Minister of Housing and Local Government on 28 September 1962 proposing a route from Eastbourne to the West Sussex county boundary near East Harting and Buriton. This route was to be available to both walkers and horse-riders. The proposal was approved without modification by Sir Keith Joseph, then Minister of Housing and Local Government, on 29 March 1963. This route was the first long-distance bridleway approved under Section 51 of the National Parks and Access to the Countryside Act of 1949.

The South Downs Way was officially opened by Lord Shawcross on 15 July 1972. It had in the meantime acquired an alternative beginning, a footpath following the cliffs through some of the finest coastal scenery of the south coast, over Beachy Head and through the Seven Sisters Country Park to the Cuckmere valley, and from there over the hills above Exceat to join the original bridleway route near Alfriston. The whole of the South Downs Way, both footpath and bridleway, is within the Sussex Downs Area of Outstanding Natural Beauty.

The Way is not a new path or bridleway. The greater part of it was already in existence when the Special Committee deliberated on the subject in 1947, and indeed as an ancient trackway was of immemorial age. The work of the Countryside Commission has been to designate the route as a long-distance way and to ensure that there is uninterrupted access for horse and man along the whole length of the bridleway. To this end local authorities acting for the Commission have where necessary negotiated new rights of way and the alteration of footpaths to bridleways.

The Commission have also arranged with the county councils for the waymarking of the route. This waymarking takes the form of concrete indicator 'plinths' or wooden signposts at junctions and intersections or at other doubtful points, the plinths or signs in most instances bearing the Commission's long-distance route symbol, an acorn. Rarely, a plaque showing the acorn is attached to a post or a stile as a confirmation of the route.

The intention of the Commission is to guide the traveller adequately without mollycoddling him, but the waymarking policies of East and West Sussex County Councils differ. East Sussex relies mostly on concrete 'plinths' and waymarks rather sparingly. In West Sussex reliance has been placed on signposts with the words 'South Downs Way' impressed on the wooden arms, together with the acorn symbol. Here every junction of the Way with a road, footpath, or bridleway is adequately signposted, so that only the unobservant could take the wrong direction. One could say that the West Sussex County Council does take the traveller by the hand and conduct him with care. Except for one curious fact. While the lettering of the words 'South Downs Way' is branded in the wood of the arms of the signposts, arms pointing to other paths are in many instances left blank, so that they do no more than indicate the existence of a track or bridleway.

Some parts of the route run for long distances without stile or gate. Others have stiles and cattle-grids, with bridle-gates or field gates for riders. There is no obstruction for riders, but they may have to dismount to open gates. Some gates will be found to be self-closing. This action is generally achieved by weights suspended on chains. The study of these weights is an amusing if minor exercise in detection. They include war-time iron shell-cases, clock pendulums, and many amorphous or intricately shaped and superannuated lumps of iron that may yield identification to a farmer old enough to have a long memory.

The uplands are divided into sections by the river valleys and by the larger 'bottoms' such as that of Jevington. In some degree the sections each possess an individuality of their own. In general the eastern blocks are high, airy, and open, and the chalk is evident in the surface of the track. West of the Arun there is much more woodland, sometimes marching with the Way for long distances; while over Graffham Down the Way runs enclosed between trees for many miles, with no view other than what may be seen in an occasional clearing. In the woodlands, and almost everywhere that trees shade or overhang the path, the overlying clay lies underfoot, mixed with humus. In dry weather it is soft and powdery, in wet weather it is muddy and in places transformed by hooves into clinging mire.

How the downs were made

The formation of the South Downs must be understood in relation to the geological development of an area comprising the Weald and the North and the South Downs as a whole. The story begins many millions of years ago with volcanoes and earth movements forming a platform of Palaeozoic rocks. In succeeding eras this platform acted as the foundation for a series of sedimentary deposits, which, under the influence of time and of great pressure, were consolidated into strata of rocks. The earliest of these strata we need consider were derived from the waters of a great freshwater lake. This lake was fed by great rivers that brought down deposits of sands and clays that spread over the bottom. These strata of sands and clays are known as the Wealden series.

After this the land slowly sank and the sea flowed in and covered the area. New and different deposits were laid down. First came the sands of the upper and lower greensand, and then came a layer of gault clay.

There now came a major change in the nature of the sea, probably connected with a rise in temperature. Chalk began to be laid down as thick sediments, and as the millennia passed these were of increasing purity. The upper Cretaceous period endured for a very long time and the beds of chalk that were laid down were hundreds of metres thick.

The chalk was derived from several sources. Much of it came from the shells of minute creatures called Foraminifera, which lived in myriads in the waters of a warm sea. As they ended their brief lives they sank to the bottom, where their soft bodies dissolved away, leaving the detritus of their shells to contribute to the future stratum of chalk. Many larger shelled creatures suffered a similar fate. Possibly some chemical processes producing calcium carbonate were also present in the formation of the chalk.

The Cretaceous period came to an end with the Eocene and yet further changes in the nature of the deposits, which were once again of sands and clays. These covered the chalk to a considerable depth.

The long period of peaceful deposition came to an abrupt end with vast earth movements that raised the Alps in central Europe and buckled and folded both recent and ancient rocks into mountain ranges. In the Wealden district they pushed up from below and distorted the sedimentary deposits into an extensive dome, 217 kilometres long from the Bas Boulonnais in France to the Hampshire

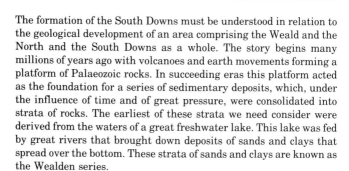

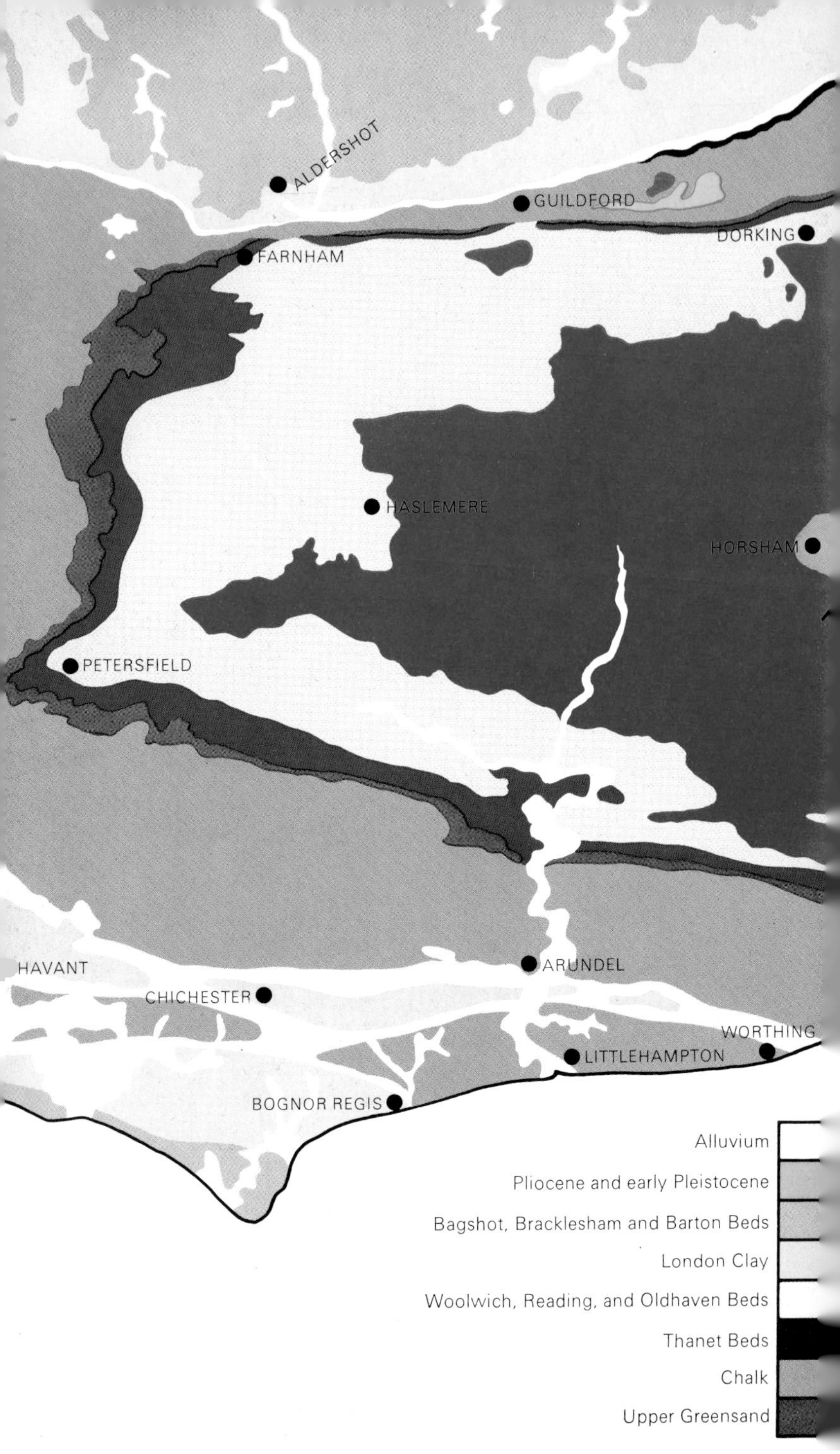
ALDERSHOT
GUILDFORD
DORKING
FARNHAM
HASLEMERE
HORSHAM
PETERSFIELD
HAVANT
CHICHESTER
ARUNDEL
WORTHING
LITTLEHAMPTON
BOGNOR REGIS
Alluvium
Pliocene and early Pleistocene
Bagshot, Bracklesham and Barton Beds
London Clay
Woolwich, Reading, and Oldhaven Beds
Thanet Beds
Chalk
Upper Greensand

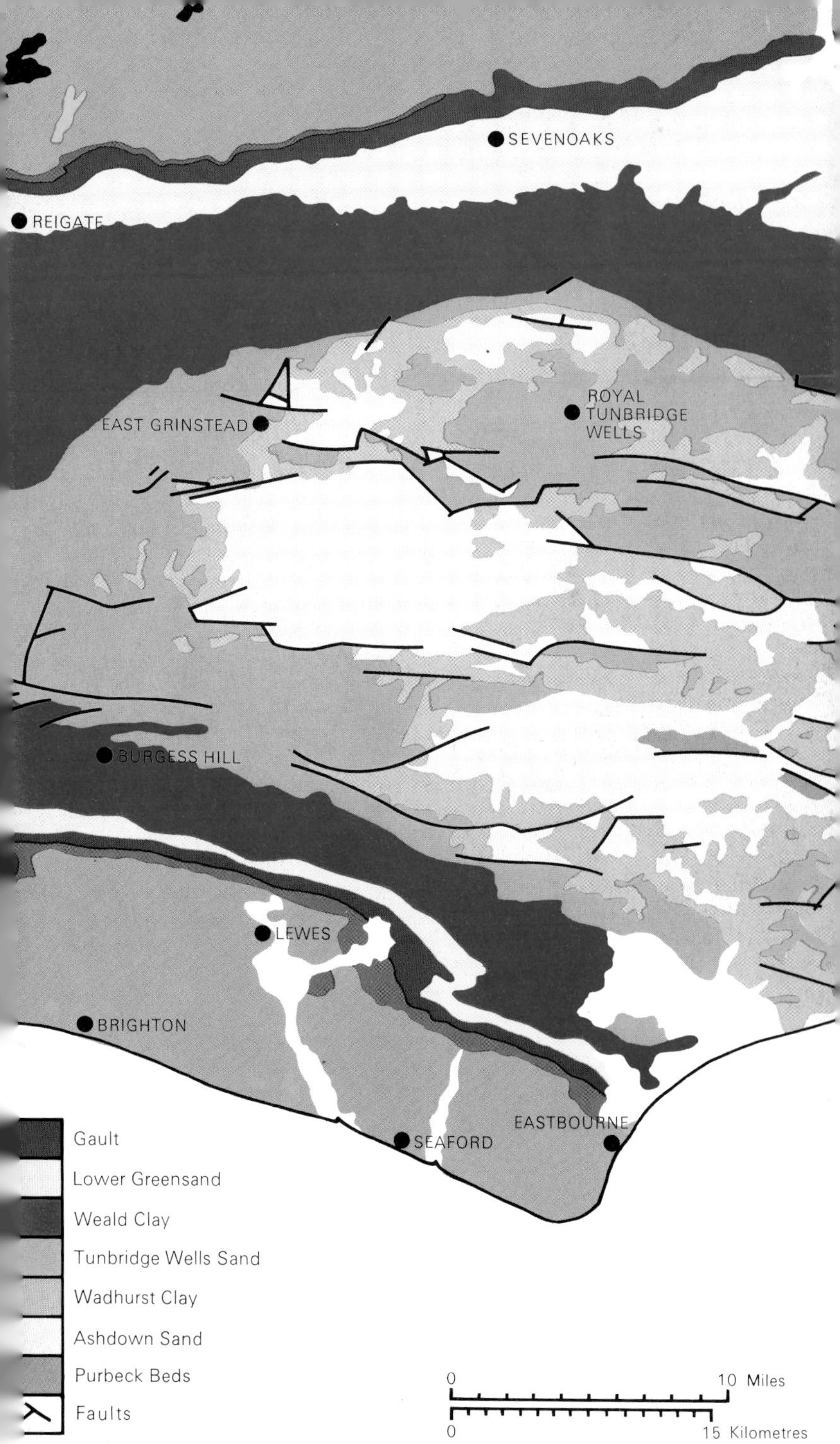
SEVENOAKS
REIGATE
EAST GRINSTEAD
ROYAL TUNBRIDGE WELLS
BURGESS HILL
LEWES
BRIGHTON
SEAFORD
EASTBOURNE
Gault
Lower Greensand
Weald Clay
Tunbridge Wells Sand
Wadhurst Clay
Ashdown Sand
Purbeck Beds
Faults
0
10 Miles
0
15 Kilometres

Downs, and 80 kilometres wide from what is now the south coast to and beyond the North Downs.

The sedimentary strata were now clear of the sea and exposed to the erosive action of the wind and the rain and of the streams and rivers that carried the rain away. That action was more powerful and persistent at the centre of the dome, which was probably riven and fissured, than it was at the edges, and in course of time the chalk of the centre was eroded. The elements then attacked the less resistant Weald clays and sands underneath.

The picture of our present landscape emerges. The central chalk and its overlying Eocene sands and clays have vanished and all that remains of the former dome are its worn-down outer slopes, which are now the North and South Downs. The evidence of this lies in the downs themselves, which present their abrupt scarp slopes towards the centre and their gentler dip slopes towards the outside. Our noble downs, north and south, are but a remnant of a much greater structure.

Within the Weald the land was not made level. There are many undulations, as for example the Forest Ridge at Horsham, and Leith Hill, which in fact rises to a greater height than any part of the downs.

The incursion of the sea to form the English Channel breached the chalk hills and exposed high and sheer cliffs as at Beachy Head and the Seven Sisters. Here the present thickness of the chalk is well demonstrated.

The river valleys

It is notable that the South Downs are divided into blocks by the valleys of rivers flowing north to south, which seem miraculously to have cut through the higher chalk country. The valleys are those of the Cuckmere, the Ouse, the Adur, and the Arun. The rivers began to flow when the dome was raised and continued in the same direction as the dome was eroded away, channelling their course as they went, so that in fact the way through the chalk downs was always cut from a higher level.

It is apparent that the rivers have been much wider than they now are, as the broad floors of their valleys, seen clearly from the neighbouring hills, demonstrate. The Cuckmere formed a silted estuary at its mouth and then cut a classic example of meanders through it.

There are several examples in the downs of river valleys that contain no river, as for example at Jevington and Saddlescombe. The dry valley is a common phenomenon of chalk country. Rivers or streams must once have flowed through these valleys, and indeed in times of abundant rain they sometimes do so again. At some time in the past the water-table in the chalk must have been considerably higher, forcing rain to run off as streams. This might have been the case in a wetter period or alternatively in the intense cold of the ice ages, when frost would have closed the porosities in the chalk and melting water would have flowed off on the surface.

The lack of water on the hills in historic times has kept them almost entirely free of settlement and even of farms. Although the

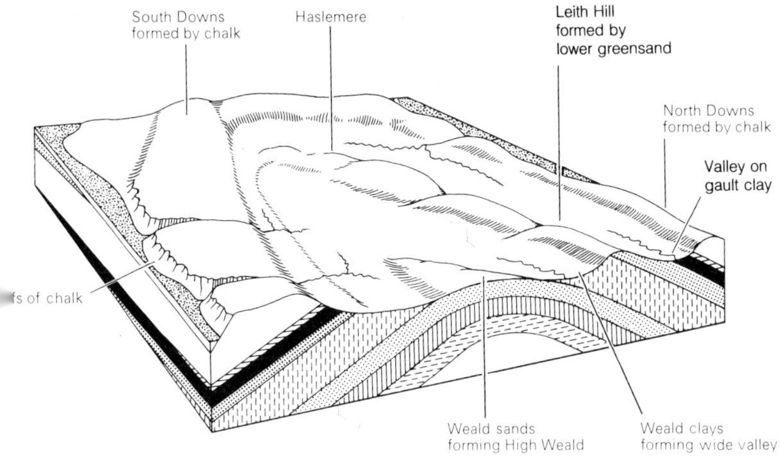

The western end of the Weald: gault, greensands and Wealden beds beneath chalk

downs have always offered attractive economic advantages as arable land or sheep country, the need for water has kept farms and villages to the spring line at the foot of the hills. Here the gault clay beneath the chalk forms an impermeable layer that forces to the surface water percolating down through the chalk.

Flint

A walk along the downs will reveal the presence of vast quantities of flints in the surface soil of fields and tracks. Flint is composed of silica, a substance of extreme hardness, with a tendency to break with sharp edges that made it highly useful to primitive man for the fashioning of tools and weapons. Its origin is not certain. It may be composed, among other things, of the dissolved spicules of sponges. That it was once liquid is apparent from the manner in which it has flowed around and enclosed fossils, and this same liquidity is possibly the cause of many curious shapes in which flint occurs. As a liquid it may have flowed into spaces in the chalk and other strata formed by the protean bodies of jellyfish or similar creatures. Flint is found in regular horizontal layers in the chalk, as may be seen in the exposed chalk cliffs of the coast. It varies in quality at different levels, as primitive man found — his mining activities for suitable qualities of flint still show in the ground, as on Cissbury Hill.

The many nodules of flint littering the hill-tops are the remains of the strata of chalk and clay that once overlaid the present uplands. As these strata were eroded, the insoluble flints collected on the surface, together with some of the clay in which they lay, forming a layer that geologists call 'clay with flints'.

South Downs Way through the ages

The designation of the South Downs Way as a long-distance route for walkers and riders is the most recent event in a long story: for the Way itself is very ancient. When we tread the chalk uplands we follow in the steps of primitive men who through thousands of generations lived by gathering, grubbing, and hunting with nothing more than simple tools to help them, and of a series of their successors who gradually developed a better culture. On the lonely hills we may feel, or imagine that we may feel, the ambience of these distant men, and though we should run from them if we saw them, we would nonetheless have to recognise in them the progenitors of ourselves.

The Old Stone Age

The Old Stone Age occupied an immense length of time, beginning long before Britain became an island. Men were free to wander from the Continent over the land that lay where the Channel now flows, or over the marshes that were what is now the North Sea. In their unceasing search for food, palaeolithic men certainly came to Britain, for some remains of them have been found, and it is likely that they travelled along the chalk ridges because those ridges would provide drier and easier going than the forested and swampy lower lands. There would have been ample small game for their sustenance and they could when they wished descend to the forests to hunt bigger game — deer, wild cattle, perhaps elephants. These men were armed only with crude stone weapons, so crude that the 'eoliths' found in Kent and attributed to them can never with certainty be distinguished from naturally occurring broken flints such as you may pick up along the South Downs Way. But they were not shambling ape-like creatures; they were positively men, and they knew the use of fire and must have possessed speech. As the centuries rolled by there was a development in their skills and their thought and they began to produce large tools (which may be seen in many museums) skilfully chipped out of flint nodules — they are known as hand-axes. They also made tools and harpoon-prongs out of bone.

With the coming of the mesolithic, the Middle Stone Age, a new flint technique appeared. Flint implements became much smaller, so small that they are known as microliths — tiny, delicate barbed arrow-heads and spear-heads that could only have been used bound to wooden hafts.

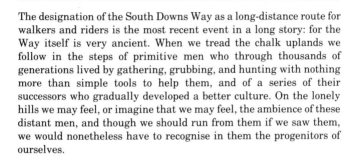

However, the evidence of the presence of palaeolithic and mesolithic men in Britain is slight. In fact, there could have been only a few hundred of them in the whole country.

The New Stone Age

With the New Stone Age we come to a different culture. While men undoubtedly still went hunting, they had also succeeded in domesticating various animals — cattle, sheep, swine, and probably dogs. They also tilled the soil, scratching and scoring it with stone hoes and bone or wooden digging sticks, and harvested their crops of emmer wheat with flint sickles.

Of necessity communities developed, under chiefs who were able to plan and undertake larger and more ambitious works, such as the causewayed camps they built on hill tops. These neolithic people are in fact known to archaeology as the Windmill Hill people, after the largest and best-investigated of these causewayed camps on Windmill Hill in Wiltshire.

A causewayed camp is an earthwork of circular form surrounded by a wide bank and ditch, with the ditch interrupted by undug causeways that give convenient access to the interior. This easy access demonstrates that these camps were not built for defence, as the later hill-forts were. It has been conjectured that they were cattle enclosures to which the herds could be driven for marking or in the autumn for culling, when a proportion of beasts had to be slaughtered for lack of winter feed — a necessity that was to apply down to the seventeenth century. Or possibly they were market-places, to which travelling pedlars brought various goods — stone axes from Graig Lwyd in Wales, gold from Ireland, trinkets for the women. There were causewayed camps on the downs on Combe Hill above Jevington, at Whitehawk near Brighton (now under the racecourse), and on the Trundle at Goodwood.

The women wove baskets of grass or rushes and from the necessity of containing the milk from their cattle and sheep they made pottery bowls, of good quality, with rounded bottoms. The men mined for flint to make tools and weapons, sinking innumerable shafts at Cissbury, on Church Hill at Findon, at Blackpatch, and perhaps on Windover Hill, and in places deep or dimpled hollows remain where the shafts were. Each shaft was filled in with the upcast from the next. From the flints they made axes, arrow-heads, and many scraper tools, which perhaps they used for scraping skins for clothing — though it is possible that their women had learned to spin and weave the wool from their sheep.

Neolithic men buried their dead under long barrows — or at least their important dead — for while there might be more than one body under a long barrow, the building of such an earthwork — some are 60 metres long — implied communal labour, which would not be available for humble men. There are a dozen long barrows in Sussex, most of them on the eastern downs — for example on Windover Hill. Today they are mere grassy mounds, not very high, but in their time they were structures of shining white chalk 3 metres high or more, flanked by ditches from which the material was dug. The barrow was set on the brow of a hill, from which point it could dominate all around.

Reconstruction of an Iron Age farmstead at the Weald and Downland Open-Air Museum

The Bronze Age

The Bronze Age did not begin suddenly as with an invasion and conquest. Rather, about the year 2000 B.C. it began to infiltrate into Britain, possibly with the stock-in-trade of merchants from Gaul, who peddled the new material to a wandering population along the downs, a population who until then had used nothing but stone or bone, the latter for only a few implements. They might already have seen copper or gold from Ireland as very rare and marvellous, but here was something more serviceable for tools and weapons.

Some bronze tools and weapons came with the arrival of a tall, long-headed people who made their way inland along the chalk ridges. They brought with them the custom of burying their dead in round barrows, a custom that was to persist down to Saxon times. Beside the body they placed a pottery drinking vessel or beaker, which has given these people the name of Beaker Folk. Their barrows lie scattered over high country from the south coast to Scotland. There are nearly a thousand round barrows in Sussex, nearly all on the downs. Originally perhaps 6 metres high, these barrows have been worn down by time until some are scarcely perceptible, while others rise still to one or two metres. All have been opened by thieves or amateur antiquaries, the latter from the seventeenth and eighteenth centuries onwards; invariably these men dug in from the top and left the barrow with a hole in the middle, like a doughnut. Many barrows have vanished in the ploughing campaigns that have changed the face of the downs since the Second World War, but they remain on the map — the Ordnance Survey calls them 'tumuli'.

These people believed in an after-life, for such a belief must underlie the inclusion of the beaker, and later of a larger food vessel and what is called an incense jar, with the body under the barrow, as it also explains the inclusion of such things as a spear-head, or a bronze dagger, and the custom of trussing up the body in a crouching position with its knees under its chin; perhaps this should be explained as a foetal attitude adopted for the return of the body to Mother Earth. A round barrow at Hove yielded, uniquely, a cup of red amber apparently turned on a lathe; it is now in the Brighton museum. Sometimes objects buried with the dead were deliberately broken, as though these should be 'dead' also. A barrow on Combe Hill above Jevington contained four bronze daggers broken in two along their length.

As the Bronze Age wore on some kind of change in religious concept came about, which was reflected in the increasing custom of incinerating the body before burial. The ashes were placed in an urn or simply heaped on the ground with the urn inverted over them, and the barrow piled on top. Cremation, however, did not destroy the after-life, for the food vessel continued to be buried with the ashes.

What we know of the Beaker Folk and their successors comes largely from interpretation of their graves and grave goods. We have little information of how they lived on or in the neighbourhood of the South Downs. On Plumpton Plain a later, and Celtic, Bronze-Age people established a small settlement. They built round huts with conical thatched roofs supported by a central pole, probably very like the huts of the model Iron-Age farm recently built on Butser Hill. The huts were surrounded by earthen banks and near them were banked cattle enclosures. The settlement was a farm and around it were square fields outlined by lynchets, fields of the type that have come to be called 'Celtic'. Such fields are identified on the Ordnance Survey maps as 'field systems'.

Although the Butser Hill project applies particularly to the Iron Age, many of its implications may be extended back in time, for there was probably little difference between the early Iron-Age and the Bronze-Age modes of life. The Butser project is a reconstruction of a farm settlement on a site anciently in use, comprising two round, thatched huts as living quarters with associated storage-pits and fields in which ancient varieties of wheat and other plants are grown by primitive methods, and sheep and cattle are bred, representing the kinds of animal shown by recovered bones to have existed at that time. The project is open to the public in the summer months.

The people of the Bronze Age wore ornaments of copper or gold from the Wicklow Hills of Ireland and blue faience beads from as far afield as Egypt, with amber from the Baltic and jet from the Yorkshire coast. It was possible for a man to travel long distances without harm, though he carried valuable goods. How else could the widespread trade of the Bronze Age have been pursued? The tracks along the chalk downs were frequented highways along which itinerant pedlars and bronze-smiths moved continually. Sometimes, however, there were emergencies and smiths had to bury or dump their stock-in-trade of new and old implements and weapons — eleven of these Bronze Age hoards have been found on the Sussex Downs.

The Iron Age

The Iron Age arrived in Britain about 500 B.C. principally by means of the Celts. They came aggressively, and the earlier Celts were constrained to build hill forts against the later ones. These forts, on hilltops where the slope of the hillside aided the defence, were intended as refuges in time of attack, but they were not elaborate — though nonetheless they entailed great labour. They consisted usually of a single rampart and ditch, with simple entrances. There were examples at Hollingbury, on Wolstonbury Hill, and at Highdown near Worthing, and probably Chanctonbury Ring belongs to this category.

The later groups of invaders provoked the elaboration of such forts and the building of new ones, such as that on the Caburn above Lewes, on the Trundle at Goodwood, on Old Winchester Hill, and perhaps also on the hill above the Devil's Dyke. But the finest example of such forts on the South Downs is that of Cissbury.

The Celts were well armed with tempered iron swords. They used iron for currency in the form of iron bars — they dug some of the ore for these in Sussex. They cut the famous White Horse in Wiltshire, and they *may* have cut the celebrated Long Man in the chalk above the village of Wilmington, perhaps originally as a phallic figure similar to the Cerne Abbas Giant in Dorset. If that was so, the Long Man has long since been emasculated by some more decorous generation.

It was the fate of the Celts to have to face the Roman legions. The Romans fought them dourly from fort to fort. In the end the Romans

Cissbury Ring. The disturbed ground is the result of neolithic flint-mining

won and the hill forts became disused and silent. In some instances, as at Old Sarum, by Salisbury, the Romans transferred the population to a lower site; the population of the Trundle was transferred to Chichester and possibly Old Winchester Hill was the original site of Winchester.

The Romans encouraged the growing of wheat on the downs and exported large quantities of it to the Continent. To facilitate their commerce they built roads from London to the south, one coming down through Ashdown Forest to Cliffe near Lewes, a second passing through Hassocks and Clayton to the coast at Brighton, and a third crossing the South Downs above Bignor. This third road was the one the Saxons called Stane Street because it was paved with stone. It descended to Chichester, which for the Romans was Regnum.

The rich farming country of the South Downs brought prosperity to Roman and Romanised farmers and there were many villas on or near the downs. The term villa in this context means simply a farm and most of these villas were of the simple corridor type, with all rooms opening off one corridor; but some of them had mosaic floors and some of them had central heating. Their occupants would have worshipped in various small temples, two of which have been found on the downs, one at Lancing and one within the earthwork of Chanctonbury Ring; nothing is to be seen of either of these buildings now.

The Saxons to modern times

The most important monument in Sussex of the Saxon invasion of Britain was the great fort of Anderida, built by the Romans. Few details are known of the Saxon conquest of Sussex after the Romans left. The Anglo-Saxon Chronicle says that a band led by Aelle and his three sons Cymen, Wlencing, and Cissa, landed near Selsey. They came in only three ships, so there could not have been many of them. Nevertheless, Aelle is recorded in 491 A.D. as laying siege to

Andredesceaster, the old Roman fort of Anderida at Pevensey, then held by desperate Celts. Aelle captured the fort and slew all he found in it. Apparently he treated any other Celts in Sussex in the same manner, for we hear no more of them and even their language disappeared, except for a few words and place-names — which, however, include the word 'downs', from Celtic 'dún', a fort or a hill — in many instances, of course, fort and hill were combined.

In place of Celtic place-names came Saxon descriptions. The earliest seem to be those ending in *ing,* as Lancing, the people of Wlenca, possibly the Wlencing who was Aelle's son, or Harting, the people of Heorot. In Sussex most *ing* names will be found between the downs and the sea. The *hams* came later, along the valleys and inland, while the *tons* seem to be connected with the uplands.

Saxon Sussex seems to have been a cultural backwater in which developments came later than they did elsewhere. For example, Sussex was not converted to Christianity until after 681 A.D., when St Wilfrid, driven out of his North Country diocese, retired to live in Sussex. Thereafter churches were built in every settlement of any size, and many of these survived, in whole or in part, the Norman's energetic drive to rebuild almost every Saxon church. It was perhaps because south Sussex was still regarded as unimportant that so many Saxon details remained. They are to be found in the downland churches of Arlington, Bishopstone, Clayton, Jevington, Singleton, and Sompting, as well as in many other places farther afield. The influences that preserved Saxon work equally applied to Norman work, and this included the richly ornamented church of Steyning as well as the splendid architecture of Chichester cathedral. The downland pastures, which now supported flocks of sheep, never produced the great fortunes such as were applied, for instance, in the building of the magnificent Gothic churches of East Anglia, which were founded on the backs of sheep. There was some development, however, as the Norman style gave way to Early English, but it was not widely continued and both Decorated and Perpendicular churches are rare in Sussex. Notable among the rarities are the two Decorated downland churches of Alfriston and Poynings.

In both church and domestic architecture flint early became the principal material of building, with stone for quoins and windows. Three churches avoid the necessity of stone in their towers by making the tower round: Southease, directly on the South Downs Way, and St Michael's at Lewes, and Piddinghoe.

The downs area slowly prospered and slowly developed. Sheep ranged the downs for centuries, and there was a special South Downs breed, developed by John Ellman of Glynde, who was born in 1753. Smugglers pursued their activities along the Sussex coast and ran their contraband inland through the river valleys that pierced the hills. The most serious alteration to the face of the downs came with the two world wars, and especially after the Second World War, when the plough and the combine harvester took over the old sheep ranges, and fences proliferated everywhere. Barley, oats, and wheat, root-crops and maize, ousted the sweet turf on which the sheep had fed, and only on the abrupt slopes of the scarp and of the 'bottoms' too steep for the plough, did something of the ancient appearance of the downs remain.

A variety of wild life

The ecological environments of the downs and of the valleys that intersect them are of diverse character, and these give rise to flora equally diverse. On the chalk uplands where the chalk is near the surface grow a number of plants that particularly like calcareous soils. Over large areas the chalk is blanketed by a covering of clay, which supports a variety of plants that prefer more neutral conditions. However, the clay may be acid, and then chalk-hating plants find the conditions they prefer. On the waterless downs water-loving plants are not to be found, except in such micro-environments as dew-ponds, in which you may find rushes and even water-lilies. Plants that flourish in damp conditions find their world in the broad valleys of the Cuckmere, the Ouse, the Adur, and the Arun.

The many woods along the Way provide yet another kind of environment, for plants that flourish in shade and in a soil enriched by leaf humus.

Finally there are the coasts and the influence of the sea. Maritime conditions pertain along the footpath from Eastbourne to the Cuckmere valley and their influence is felt farther inland along the high downs.

The cliffs provide a fusion of marine coast and chalk downs. The plants here are mostly low or are excessively dwarfed by the conditions. Frequent among the grass shines the beautiful blue of viper's bugloss. Here too you may find a dwarfed variety of the carline thistle, whose yellow flower is dry, like an *immortelle*. The blue, star-like petals of the spring squill may catch your eye in April or June, and those of the autumn squill in August. On Beachy Head there are solid thickets of small trees and bushes that include dogwood, elder, varieties of willow, and raspberries and blackberries, here and there thickly cloaked with travellers' joy and ivy.

The two plants most characteristic of the chalk downs may be said to be the beech tree and travellers' joy. In places the beech forms dense woods and covers the ground beneath its spreading branches with a rich, rusty carpet. There is little light in a beech-wood and many plants will not grow there. Among those that will are the white, starry anemone and the graceful white helleborine. The sober bird's-nest orchid seems to derive its colour from the dead, brown leaves and it does not mind deep shade. Sober too is the pale green spathe of the arum lily, surely one of the strangest of English flowers, but by no means uncommon; it is sometimes called cuckoo-pint, or lords-and-ladies, or parson-in-the-pulpit, or Adam-

and-Eve. Reticent as it may be in flower, its fruit is just the opposite, the brilliant green, yellow, and red berries gleaming on the bare stem. Not uncommon is the woodruff, whose leaves and white flowers contain coumarin and smell of vanilla or new-mown hay.

The ploughing of the downs has reduced or destroyed the habitats of many downland plants and the use of weed-killers has prevented the growth of many colourful weeds that made the corn gay, though they dismayed the farmer. Poppies no longer form sheets of red in the cornfields, but they may still be seen along the margins and the hedgerows. The places to look for wild plants on the downs are along the paths themselves, where Germander speedwell, pineapple mayweed (which smells of pineapples), and basil thyme in many places form a thick, crisp carpet; along the uncultivated slopes of the bottoms and the scarps, which are inaccessible to the plough; on barrows and earthworks, where the ground may not have been disturbed for two or three thousand years (unless by archaeologists and robbers); along the hedgerows and along the wire fences that are more common than hedgerows; and on the few hilltops, such as Windover Hill, that have not recently been subjected to the plough; and even along the verges of the few lengths of surfaced road that, perforce, the Way must follow — some of these verges, as that between Southease and Rodmell, exhibit a surprising variety of plants and bushes.

Among the most frequent of plants is knapweed, whose unfortunate name is attached to a charming plant with a delicate purple flower. The stems of knapweed are remarkably tough and resist the grazing of animals. Also very common everywhere, and resistant to grazing because it is unpalatable, is ragwort, thrusting, untidy plants with bright yellow flowers. Unpalatable, even slightly poisonous though they may be, they are the food preferred by the black and yellow banded caterpillars of the cinnabar moth. The lilac heads of scabious are also frequent on the chalk and on the clay, modestly displaying their charms. A flower that at first glance may be mistaken for a scabious is the round-headed rampion, which prefers the chalk, but its curly head and stronger colour and its lanceolate leaves distinguish it. The rampion is a member of the bellflower family and the pretty clustered bellflower itself also decorates the chalk uplands with its purple bells. The rather paler purple of the nettle-leaved bellflower will be found in the woods. A distant relative, Venus's looking-glass, has more open, and smaller, purple flowers, but as the flowers tend to close at the first hint of dull weather, it is not always easy to see in the grass.

Cowslips used to be common on the downs and may still be found in April and May, perhaps with oxlips. Yellow is repeated in the grasslands by the multifarious hawkbits and hawkweeds, whose flowers, resembling dandelions, may be distinguished by the square-cut or knicked ends to the petals. The pappus — the green cup beneath the flower — of some of them produces a clock.

Perhaps no such clock is as handsome as that of the goatsbeard, backed by the sword-like spikes of its sepals. The plant is not common but may be found in the hedgerows on the chalk.

One of the plants that scents the air of the downs is salad burnet, which, with compound leaves like those of silverweed, and petal-less

Marbled white butterflies with bird's-foot trefoil

flowers coloured by red stiles and yellow stamens, smells of cucumber. A relative of this is agrimony whose spikes of yellow flowers rise frequently from the turf of the chalk. Wild mignonette is seen but is less common than weld, whose spikes of pale yellow flowers will be found along many parts of the Way in July and August. Another yellow spike is that of toadflax, whose flowers, of snapdragon form, appear from May to October.

Among the herbs growing along the Way will be found basil thyme, spreading its violet flowers low underfoot, so tiny that a close look is required to see the characteristic white mark on the lower lip;

it flowers from June to September. Wild thyme is another prostrate plant flowering at the same time. Marjoram, on the other hand, flourishes to a height of about a metre, spreading its purple flowers in untidy umbels.

Thistles grow almost anywhere, though perhaps the stemless thistle likes the hill slopes. On the other hand, there are giant thistles like triffids that spring man-high out of the corn.

Many orchids may be found along the Way; by no means all of them are rare. The bee orchid, whose flower looks like a large bumble bee busily sucking nectar, is specific to lime and chalk, but is not common. The military orchid is extremely rare and many botanists have never seen one. The pyramidal orchid is more common and may be known by its pyramid of pink flowers in June to August, and perhaps by its smell, which is said to be foxy. The fragrant orchid is similar but with a more attractive scent.

Over a distance of more than 100 kilometres of countryside there are bound to be baleful or poisonous plants. Chief among these, with a rich, round, glossy black berry that seems to ask to be eaten, is deadly nightshade, a gawky plant reaching a metre or so high, with purplish bellflowers that grow at the same time as the berries. A lane full of these plants is found above Buriton. Also called dwale and belladonna, the whole plant is highly poisonous; leave it alone. Bittersweet is an unhappy but apparently descriptive name for woody nightshade, the poisonous plant whose brightly coloured, egg-shaped berries hang in bunches, often among blackberries; they come from purple flowers with a prominent column of yellow anthers; their form proclaims their connection with the potato and the tomato.

A variety of bushes will be found along the Way. Travellers' joy is frequent; unable to support itself, it clambers over and strangles other bushes. Its feathery grey plumes in autumn give it the name of old man's beard. Ivy is almost as frequent, with the same climbing habit; notice how its leaves change shape with height — triple-lobed low down, much simpler higher up. The coarse, strongly veined leaves of dogwood contrast with the small, smooth leaves of the sloe, otherwise called the blackthorn, whose white blossoms, coming on the naked bough, are among the first to appear in spring. Hawthorn is plentiful, with its creamy blossoms richly scented in May or June, its red berries bright in autumn; and so too is elder, its great, heavy disks of white blossom smelling of cats and turning to rafts of glossy black berries. Both blossom and berries make excellent wine, a white wine from the blossom, a deep red from the berries.

The spindle tree is not common, but it is a native of the chalk. Its inconspicuous greenish flowers produce handsome multi-seeded coral berries so curious in form that they are not likely to be mistaken. Juniper sprawls on the hills, its black berries smelling of gin. Purging buckthorn flourishes on chalk, its boldly veined leaves and black berries making it distinctive. Sea buckthorn is a very different bush, armed with ferocious spines; its normal habitat is near the sea, but in some instances the South Downs are near enough for it — I found it on Cissbury. The brimstone butterfly feeds on the leaves. Honeysuckle, richly and sweetly scented, with an odd and beautiful flower, climbs over hawthorn and sloe. Gorse or furze grows in great clumps, which are evergreen; the yellow flowers have a long season but are at their most brilliant in June. Various kinds of wild roses give double delight to the eye, with their flowers in early summer and their scarlet hips in autumn.

Among trees the king of the chalk is certainly the beech, which grows to noble dimensions in woodland, with its massive grey, smooth boles and far-spreading branches; no tree, unless it is the lime, has a lovelier and more delicate green of the spring leaf. Sometimes, as at Buriton, the woods form steep hangers on hill slopes. Ash is common, both as an isolated tree and in plantations. Oaks appear in the lower land. Yews do well on chalk but they are not numerous along the South Downs Way; there are stands of them a little south of the Way, in Kingly Vale south of the Devil's Jumps. Sycamores multiply by means of their twirling keys, and so too do their relatives the maples, which are found in leafy lanes. Whitebeam and lime occur in the valleys, where, too, there is a flora different from that of the hills. One of the most decorative plants of the valleys is the mallow, of which there are two varieties, the common and the dwarf; they like to be near water, but not necessarily near enough to have their feet wet; you will find examples round Exceat.

Birds

The habitats for birds are as varied as for plants. Gulls and terns, the latter as swift and graceful as swallows, will be seen along the coast and far up the rivers, where various ducks and waders may also be found. In close weather, swifts, martins, and swallows come low to quarter the downs at high speed, among the most graceful and agile of birds; but not too fast or too agile to be caught on the wing by the hobby falcon, which itself has an outline, in flight, similar to that of a swift.

From the high heavens the sober-suited skylark pours out a cascade of song. Another singer from the heights is the meadow pipit or titlark, which ceases its song abruptly to drop like a stone to the earth and its eggs, so thickly scribbled over as to be almost solid black. Less elevated performers, the chaffinch, the blackbird, and the thrush will sing sweetly from a post or the branch of a bush. In the woods the nightingale may be heard, not necessarily at night.

Also in the woods the goldcrest flutters brightly from conifer to conifer, and though the smallest of British birds, it has little fear of man. The tree-creeper and the nuthatch walk up and down tree-trunks as though gravity did not exist for them. Woodpeckers hammer the bark with a machine-gun rattle. The round and rosy bullfinch walks along the branches of flowering shrubs picking out the blossoms. The goldfinch haunts the woodland rides and the hedges, dipping its scarlet head.

Out in the open the magpie lumbers in evening dress to a brief dinner in the fields, and by his size momentarily frightens smaller birds. They take more serious notice of the gliding or hovering outline of a kestrel or a sparrowhawk, which rouses pigeons to a noisy departure.

The harsh voice of the corncrake may be heard from the corn, and in the evening the churr of the nightjar — but nightjars, almost

Kestrel (male) with female hovering

invisible on the ground, so effective a camouflage is their plumage, are not now very common; they nest in the corn and the early cutting of the harvest that is modern practice militates against their increase.

You may, in the open, see the fat, rounded form of a quail, but they are not common. You will almost certainly see partridge, but you will need to be close to distinguish whether they are the common or the red-legged kind. Pheasants I am sure you will find, for these large, semi-domesticated birds are locally common.

An owl by day is likely to be mobbed by smaller birds and it would rather hide away; but at night you may glimpse owls and you will hear their calling.

You are most unlikely to see a great bustard. According to the naturalist Gilbert White, these huge and handsome birds roamed the downs near Brighton. Up to $1\frac{1}{4}$ metres high and with a wing-span of 2 metres, they could both run and fly swiftly, but because they needed large areas of scrubland and because they provided excellent meat, they became extinct throughout the country. An attempt has been made to re-establish them on Porton Down in Wiltshire, and who knows, you might meet a stray in its old haunts.

Animals

Rabbits are the animals you are most likely to see, either in the woods or on the open downs. Hares perhaps come next; you are most likely to encounter them as the dusk comes down, when you may see them ahead of you on the path, standing upright and listening with long ears erect. Since there are rabbits and hares there are also foxes, which find plenty of secure hiding-places in the woods and in the scrub. Moles have a liking for clay over chalk, for it breeds fat worms, on which the mole lives; old and recent molehills are evidence of his long lease of the downs. Deer are probably present in the extensive woods such as Charlton Forest, but I have not seen any. Stoats track their prey relentlessly through the undergrowth and frighten a doomed rabbit into a screaming cry. Their smaller

Badger

Adder

cousins, weasels, live off rats, mice, and other small game, and may steal birds' eggs from nests; they themselves are prey for hawks and owls.

Rats, voles, and various kinds of mice are numerous but are mostly creatures of the night, as are shrews.

The red squirrel is absent, displaced by his grey cousin, which, confident in his impudence or his speed, will let you see him, but if alarmed, soon puts a tree between you and him. Badgers announce their presence by their massive excavations, but they are nocturnal creatures.

Frogs, which are amphibious animals, may be seen in the river valleys, but not on the dry downs, where toads also seldom come.

Reptiles

Snakes, lizards, and slow-worms should all be present but are seldom seen. There is a sign at the foot of Cissbury Ring warning of adders, but unless stepped on or interfered with, adders are inoffensive creatures that would rather beat a retreat than try a contest with a human being. They are easily distinguished, by the V on the head and the zigzag down the back, from the venomless grass snake and the slow-worm; but if you pick up either a grass snake or a slow-worm it may show its displeasure by biting.

The common lizard likes to bask in the sun and may choose a path for a sun-bath. It will quickly dart away if disturbed — your footfall at a distance is sufficient to send it into hiding. If you grab one by the tail it will leave its tail in your hand: this is no old wives' story — the wriggling tail in your hand and the bleeding stump disappearing into the bushes will make you wish you had not tried the experiment.

Insects

The paths along the downs are visited by a variety of butterflies. Among the most frequent are the fritillaries, richly spotted on an orange or brownish base colour. The silver-washed fritillary and the Queen of Spain will be seen in the neighbourhood of woods. The Duke of Burgundy likes to lay its eggs on primroses and cowslips. The tortoiseshells are not uncommon and the peacock may be seen. The elegant marbled white is distinctive, and so too is the grayling, which may be seen on nettles. Many small brown butterflies are found, and these include the rapid little skippers, the darkest of which, coming in spring, is appropriately called the 'dingy skipper'.

A butterfly you may look for in vain is the delicate and rare chalk-hill blue, with blue body and brown-marked blue wings, the under-sides of which are quite different from the upper. The pretty little orange tip is more frequent, and who could possibly mistake the brimstone-yellow, with a single orange spot on each wing?

There are many beetles. Ladybirds of many varieties are common. The fearsome (but harmless) stag-beetle seems to be always lethargic, exhausted by the weight of its own horns. The use of the Way by horses means that there is dung, which attracts certain species of beetle. Cow-dung also has its beetle gourmets. Both dungs also attract yellow dung-flies.

Dragonflies dart and hover with wings vibrating so fast as to be almost invisible; some people think that there is a sting in that long tail, but what they mistake for a sting is an oviposter. Damsel-flies resembling dragonflies, may be seen over water; they fly with flapping wings, as a butterfly does.

Bumble-bees make themselves busy in the hedges and among the meadow flowers; their Latin title *Bombus* suits their shape, as 'bumble' suits their flight. Grasshoppers in summer keep up a constant chirrup in the grass.

There are too many insects for more than a few to be mentioned. An entomologist with a magnifying glass will find dense populations along the South Downs Way.

Farming on the South Downs

In 1938 A. E. Trueman, in his *Scenery of England and Wales,* could say that on the South Downs, because of the thin covering of soil, sheep-farming was almost universal. Between then and now, despite the thinness of the soil covering, the picture has changed utterly. Any walker or rider travelling the length of the South Downs Way will find that farming on the South Downs is overwhelmingly arable.

It is not the first time the South Downs have grown grain. The Romans derived large quantities of grain from the downs, and during the Napoleonic wars large areas were given over to arable. In neither instance, however, was the use of the downs for arable as great as it is today. The cause of today's superiority is found in the great advance of farm machinery, notably the tractor-driven plough and the combine harvester. The plough has driven deep into the shallow soil, biting into the chalk beneath (and incidentally creating myriads of broken chalk fragments to join the ever-present flints), and the combine harvester can clear enormous areas in a day, cutting a swathe 5 metres wide.

Vast fields, in which machines can work unhindered by walls and fences, are the most economical for modern farm machinery. The fields found on the downs today *are* vast, divided almost everywhere only by light fences of posts and barbed wire. Even so, farmers often sow the same crop in two or three fields together.

Three-quarters of the crops grown in England are cereals; the proportion on the South Downs may be higher. But cereals cannot be grown year after year on the same ground; a rotation is practised to keep the land in good heart. The largest crop is barley, used principally for animal foodstuffs and brewing. Wheat is grown for flour and again for animal foodstuffs; wheat sown in winter, in October or November, is ready for harvest in late summer or early autumn. Oats are also grown for foodstuffs. Rye is seldom seen. Grass and clover may be grown for silage. Various root crops will be found as also fields of beans and of maize.

The flocks of sheep that made the South Down breed famous no longer range freely on the hills, but sheep are not entirely absent.

The most frequent breed of cattle is the black and white Friesian, which is popular because it is a good beast for milk.

Comparatively minor uses of the land are for forestry — the Forestry Commission have extensive woods, especially in the western part of the downs — and for breeding game; pheasants may be seen frequently, especially near Bignor.

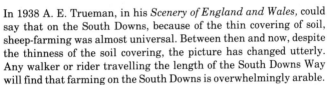

On the Way

Walkers

Stalwarts who think nothing of 30 kilometres in a day will cover the South Downs Way in less than a week, but to do this they will need to emulate the snail by taking their house on their backs. They will also need to plan their supplies of food and especially of water. The Way passes through few villages and in general supplies will mean a detour of a kilometre or two into the Weald. Water is a rare commodity along the Way. Don't suppose that you will drink out of dew-ponds or out of farmers' cattle-troughs. Dew-ponds may dry up in warm weather, though reputation says they don't, and even where they do contain water you may be inclined, on inspection, to leave it to the cattle. The same remark applies to cattle-troughs; many of these will be found to be empty, with the ball valves that serve them covered over and locked — farmers have past experience of the depredations of some members of the public. So you must find your water where you can, perhaps in the village shops where you buy your supplies, and you must carry it with you for at least an hour or two.

For those who prefer to do the 128-kilometre journey in sections, convenient stages are marked by valleys containing railway lines or bus routes. By making use of buses and trains you may travel the whole of the Way from three centres: Eastbourne, Brighton and Chichester. On some routes buses may be infrequent, but in general you will be unfortunate to have to wait more than an hour. It is imperative to study the bus and train timetables; some services do not run on Sundays, some only on certain weekdays. Timetables for East and West Sussex buses may be obtained from Southdown Motor Services Ltd., Freshfield Road, Brighton. West Sussex County Council have published a free leaflet *South Downs Way Public Transport Guide*. It can be obtained from them at County Hall, Chichester.

I have seen people walking the Way in light shoes or even pumps. These are suitable only in settled dry weather, and even then are uncomfortable on stony ground. Strong shoes or boots are more sensible at most times of the year; they should have stout soles of the Itshide or Commando type.

In summer the tops of the downs may be very hot, with no shade of any kind for miles; then a sun-hat may be welcome. The lack of shelter applies equally when the rain falls or when sharp, cold winds blow over the ridges; then warm clothing and a cagoule with a hood,

Walkers on the Seven Sisters

or some similar wind and waterproof garment will be appreciated.

The South Downs Way provides very safe walking. There are no abrupt crags or precipices for the negligent to fall over, although take care on the crumbly Seven Sisters cliffs. There are steep slopes along the scarp, but most of these are fenced — not for your benefit, but by farmers for the protection of their cattle. You will never be very far from civilisation in the shape of a public road — any path or bridleway leading north from the Way will serve. The main peril is likely to be a wrenched or sprained ankle from one of the deep ruts or from stepping on a loose stone or flint. You should carry normal first aid items, particularly a crêpe bandage and also half a dozen plasters in case of blisters or chafed toes. A whistle to give the recognised distress signal may be useful in case of accident, as may a torch.

Riders

The whole of the South Downs Way, except for the alternative footpath section from Eastbourne to Alfriston, is open to riders as a bridleway. Except in a few instances the going is all on paths and tracks, with surfaces varying from loose flints and bare chalk with deep ruts to occasional stretches of fine turf as at Chanctonbury. It should be said, however, that there are not many stretches where a horse may go at any faster pace than a walk. Narrow furrows, which the horse must follow, or flinty or stony paths, will constrain it, and in wet weather many lengths on chalk or clay are slippery. There are a few places where it may be more advisable to lead a horse than to ride it, as down the eroded chalk track from Chanctonbury to the main road near Washington. It is not difficult for riders to cross the dual carriageway of the A24 at this point, but for those who wish to avoid it a detour has been described to the north through Washington, where there is a bridge.

It is better and more enjoyable to ride in a leisurely fashion along the Way, spending several nights out, but on a fit horse and travelling light in good weather the journey may be done in two or three days.

A horse's hooves should be newly shod before making a long journey along the Way. The use of leather soles could prevent a bruised frog, and plugs or studs will help in slippery conditions.

Farriers are few and far between, at a distance from the Way, and always busy. Riders are advised always to carry a hoof pick, and, in case of a cut by flint or wire, a tail-bandage. Water is scarce; occasionally you will find a cattle-trough, and where these are accessible without damage to crops, and the water is clean, you should allow your horse to take a few mouthfuls.

There are no trekking centres on the South Downs. Stabling or grazing and accommodation for riders can be found reasonably close to the Way, but should be booked well in advance, especially when there are two or more riders together. Ensure that feed and hay are available at overnight stops, or that you have an adequate support team, otherwise you may have to carry oats.

Detailed information of overnight stops for riders and of nearby pubs may be obtained from Mr Charles Shippam, Laybrook Farm, Goose Green, Thakeham, Pulborough, West Sussex RH20 2LN, *provided a stamped and addressed envelope is enclosed with request.*

Cyclists

The South Downs Way is officially open to cyclists, except for the alternative footpath section from Eastbourne through Exceat to Alfriston. In fact, not much of the Way is suitable for cycling and any cyclist undertaking it will have to envisage a great deal of pushing, not only up hills but over surfaces made difficult by ruts, by long grasses, by stones, and by mud.

Advice and information on cycling may be obtained from the Cyclists' Touring Club, Cotterell House, Meadrow, Godalming, Surrey GU7 3HS. Remember, courtesy demands that on bridleways cyclists, like horse-riders, give precedence when necessary to walkers.

Motorists

Cars and motor-cycles are mostly prohibited from using the Way. There are few places where they *could* use it safely. Tracks that appear promising at the beginning develop deep ruts or become narrow, or come to bridle-gates, which do not exceed 1½ metres in width and are mostly less than this.

Motorists may walk lengths of the Way by leaving their cars at points where the Way crosses a road. At most such points there is space for rough or unofficial parking, and some of these points are indicated in this guide. There is official parking at a few points where a surfaced road reaches or crosses the Way, and these too are indicated.

The weather

The fact that crops of wheat, barley, and oats are grown successfully to the tops of the downs is a measure of the general mildness of the climate of the hills over the greater part of the year. Frosts are common from November to April, but snow is neither frequent nor usually heavy, and it does not normally lie long. The annual rainfall is 1000 mm on the downs, less in the lower lands or near the sea. The average July temperature is about 21°C(70°F), and about 2°C(36°F) for January.

Accommodation

Accommodation may be found in several villages and towns mostly at some little distance from the South Downs Way, but you must not suppose that this will always be conveniently at hand nor that it will be available on casual application. There are several publications listing accommodation, some of which are given in the bibliography at the end of this book. It is advisable to reserve accommodation beforehand, making arrangements at the same time for meals.

Don't count on dropping down to a village inn for a meal or accommodation. Though they may do snacks at the bar, many pubs have no facilities for meals or accommodation.

Wild camping is possible, with the landowner's permission, in places along the South Downs, but you may have to walk some way before you find a bit of wild land suitable for a tent. There are a few places where you may camp officially; and details of these may be obtained from books listed in the bibliography.

Horse-riders require care and sustenance for their mounts as well as for themselves. Grazing and stabling are available at a number of places along the Way, and a list of these may be obtained from Mr. Charles Shippam at the address given on page 27.

There are six Youth Hostels more or less convenient for the Way:

Beachy Head
East Dean Road, Eastbourne, East Sussex BN20 8ES. Telephone Eastbourne 37294. Hostel marked 'Club House' on the 1:25,000 map, 'CH' on the 1:50,000 map. The hostel is near the beginning of both the footpath and the bridleway.

Alfriston
Frog Firle, Alfriston, Polegate, East Sussex BN26 5TT. Telephone Alfriston 423. $1\frac{1}{2}$ kilometres south of Alfriston.

Telscombe
Bank Cottages, Telscombe, Lewes, East Sussex BN7 3HZ. Telephone Brighton 37077. $3\frac{1}{4}$ kilometres south west of Southease.

Patcham
Patcham Place, Brighton BN1 8YD. Telephone Brighton 556196. $6\frac{1}{2}$ kilometres north of Brighton, 3 kilometres south of the Way.

Truleigh Hill
Tottington Barn, Truleigh Hill, Shoreham by Sea, East Sussex BN4 5FB. Telephone Steyning 813419. The hostel stands beside the South Downs Way north of Shoreham.

Arundel
Warningcamp, Arundel, West Sussex BN18 9QY. Telephone Arundel 882204. The hostel is $2\frac{1}{2}$ kilometres east of Arundel and 5 kilometres from the South Downs Way at Amberley.

It is essential to make prior booking at Youth Hostels. Details of membership can be obtained from: Youth Hostels Association, Trevelyan House, St. Albans, Hertfordshire AL1 2DY.

Eastbourne to Alfriston (footpath)

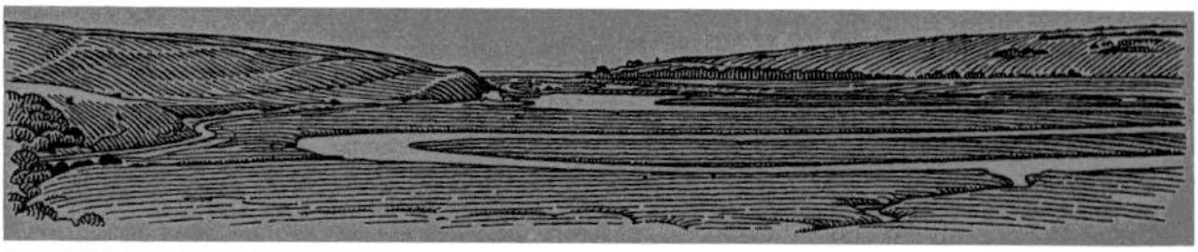

Total distance 17½ kilometres

The South Downs Way footpath begins at the edge of the downs west of Eastbourne, beyond the end of the promenade. This point may be reached by No. 6 Corporation bus from Gildredge Road opposite the railway station. There is official parking along the promenade and unofficial parking along the south side of the road beyond the promenade; also a multi-storey car park in Eastbourne.

Eastbourne to Exceat

Distance 11 kilometres

At the foot of the downs there is a refreshment kiosk. In front of it a concrete plinth, bearing an acorn and the words 'South Downs Way' with an arrow, marks the beginning of the Way. Here in 1972 the ceremony of the official opening of the Way by Lord Shawcross took place. There is a map board showing the route.

We go forward up the hill and up a flight of concrete steps in which are set a number of split flints that must have had their origin in the chalk of the downs. We pursue our direction, with the sea far below on our left, cross a mown track, and later enter a broad track bordered by a medley of bushes on both sides. We emerge above a deep hollow, Whitebread Hole, going down to the cliff edge; it has a playing field in the bottom. A South Downs Way plinth confirms that we are on the route, but seems to bear too much to the right. Our way is to maintain our altitude above the hole, and shortly another South Downs Way plinth confirms that this is correct. The path becomes a mere channel along the contour, from which it descends to go between bushes above a steep slope going down to the cliff edge. It is an interesting exercise to try to identify the species of bushes on these downs — start with hawthorn, sloe, elderberry, dogwood, furze. Beyond Heathy Brow the path becomes asphalted, a relic of the last war, when there was a radar station here.

On top of Beachy Head a small octagonal enclosure of brick, the interior lined with seats, is all that remains of a Lloyds signal station built in 1886. A cluster of buildings inland from it includes a pub and a cafeteria.

The word 'Beachy' is from the French *beau chef,* beautiful headland; the word 'head' in the English name is therefore repetitious. In one way or another, Beachy Head and the neighbouring Seven Sisters country are protected from development. Eastbourne Corporation bought 1,600 hectares in 1924, and in 1957 it

Top: Beachy
bottom: Sev
from Birlin

was given 40 hectares at Whitebread Hole. The National Trust owns over 250 hectares of the Seven Sisters, together with land at Birling Gap, and the Forestry Commission owns a large tract of land inland north of the A259 — Friston Forest. The cliffs as far as Seaford have been defined as the Sussex Heritage Coast.

The white chalk cliffs of Beachy Head, which rise 161 metres sheer from the sea, are famous for their splendour, which is continued by the undulating Seven Sisters. A walk along the top is exhilarating. Far below, the red-banded lighthouse, built in 1902, makes a picture much photographed against the cliffs that render it diminutive. It replaced the Belle Tout lighthouse, built in 1832 on the cliff to the west; Belle Tout was converted into a house before the war. The owner gave it to Eastbourne Corporation. We pass north around the wall of its enclosure, just above the road that runs to Birling Gap, and above the car parks alongside it. Beyond Belle Tout the track keeps a little inland from the cliffs and descends towards a coastguard station called the Look-Out. A great deal of viper's bugloss grows about here, and also weld, a species of wild mignonette.

The buildings of Birling Gap are seen below, and we descend to them on the landward side. There is a car park here (fee) and in summer the beach may be reached by steps.

The Way continues outside the car park up a gravelly track with a prominent sign advising no cars, parking or picnicking. A South Downs Way sign points the way forward. At the top of the track pass an iron gate and turn right, then almost immediately left and this will bring you to the open cliffs which are followed for 4½ kilometres. The route is very up and down over the rises and through the hollows of the Seven Sisters. The cliff scenery is magnificent. Notice the horizontal lines of flints in the chalk.

The first sister is Went Hill, which drops to Michel Dean. Then comes Baily's Hill, with a short obelisk on the slope, commemorating the gift of the land by W. A. Robertson to the National Trust. Next come Flat Hill, Flagstaff Bottom, and Flagstaff Point, where a sarsen stone on a plinth records the presentation of the Crowlink Valley by Viscount Gage of Firle in 1926. A bench looks out over the sea. A building inland is the Holiday Fellowship guesthouse. The following sisters are Brass Point, Rough Brow, Short Brow, and Haven Brow. The percipient will count eight sisters in this list. Flat Hill is the one excluded to make the magical (and alliterative) figure of seven.

At the top of Haven Brow we come in sight of the Cuckmere valley, extending from the beach across Cuckmere Haven up to Exceat Bridge, and see clearly the writhing meanders of the river and the straight channel cut in 1846 to by-pass those meanders and prevent flooding. Inland from the beach a bar of shingle stretches across the valley, and behind there is a raised causeway, along which the Way goes.

Before leaving Haven Brow, take a good look at Cuckmere valley. It is one of the very few havens on the south coast that has not been developed. You look upon a rarity, an unspoilt haven, with white cliffs stretching beyond it towards Seaford.

From Haven Brow follow a wire fence on the right to a stile

halfway down the hill — there is no sign. Cross the stile and descend the hill, and then go down the cliff by a very steep chalk track, at the foot of which is a South Downs Way plinth. We are at the beginning of the causeway, which leads to the east bank of the Cuckmere. Follow the straight river to Exceat Bridge, and there turn right along the footpath of the A259 to Exceat Farm.

Buses run along the A259 from Seaford to Eastbourne, stopping at Exceat Farm.

From Exceat to Alfriston

Distance 6½ kilometres

There is a large car park beside the Cuckmere opposite Exceat Farm and there is more parking among trees off the side road west of the farm.

Exceat Farm, built of flint, has been converted to an interpretive centre for the Seven Sisters Country Park and there is an interesting permanent exhibition of posters, photographs, models, stuffed birds, etc., in the barn; various publications and leaflets may be obtained here.

East of the barn we turn up a short lane to a stile. A wooden South Downs Way sign on the wall of one of the farm buildings confirms the direction. Beside the stile is a notice of the Rare Breeds Survival Trust describing their aim of preserving unusual breeds of farm animals threatened with extinction. You may see strange cattle in the field beyond the stile.

We climb straight ahead up the field, which rises steeply, with excellent views of the meanders of the Cuckmere. In the north-west corner of the field is a mysterious mound that looks like a long barrow. We come to a stile in a wall and step over it on to a stone with a bench-mark. We are now in Friston Forest, a mixed forest of not very ancient trees. The path is clearly visible. It drops down to the village of Westdean, between a pond and a house with a number of small stone sculptures. Ahead is Forge Cottage. We go up the lane beside this. If you wish to see the church, as you should, take the next turning right.

Westdean village is almost all of flint and is charming. Just below the church is a pigeon-tower and a massive lump of wall, all that remains of the manor-house of the Thomas family, who have a monument in the church. The church, also of flint, with a square tower under a Sussex cap, is of Norman origin, with details of the thirteenth, fourteenth and fifteenth centuries. It contains two modern carved heads, one of the painter Sir Oswald Birley, and the other, by Epstein, of Viscount Waverley, better known as Sir John Anderson, the politician.

Turn out of the church under the ancient yew, and notice the excellent lettering on the eighteenth-century tomb-chests in the churchyard. Notice also the thirteenth-century parsonage house by the churchyard gate, somewhat over-restored.

Return to the lane coming up from Forge Cottage. Up the hill, where the concrete path veers to the left to a house called the Glebe, we go ahead over a stile into a lane between tall bushes and trees. A few metres farther on we come to a junction and turn left, following the indication of a South Downs Way signpost of an original design, with short triangles to point the way, the first of several in this part of the forest. Bushes and trees flanking the path include hazel and larch, and soon on the right there is a tall, untrimmed hedge of cupressus, thick and graceful and set here for no apparent purpose.

Ignoring the red arrows (for a forest walk), we follow the pointing triangles of the South Downs Way signposts and come to a place where the main track and the red arrows veer right. A South Downs Way sign indicates our way ahead over a stile and we descend on a narrow path downhill through woodland. At the bottom of the hill we turn left along a plain path and soon cross a drive that leads to Charleston Manor. Unfortunately only the merest glimpse of the house is possible, except perhaps in winter. The house is of Norman origin and it stands in a beautiful garden. It was the home of Sir Oswald Birley, the painter whose sculptured head we saw in Westdean church. The house is open to the public, but the grounds are entered from the other side.

Passing over the drive we follow a narrow path, and very soon, at a South Downs Way plinth, turn sharply right over a barway stile — a

Cattle from Rare Breeds Survival Trust: Highland (top) and White Park

The meandering Cuckmere from Exceat

barway is a gap closed by three or four horizontal poles or planks. We now follow on rising ground along the margin of cornfields. Pass through three fields and in the corner of the third field take a stile left and immediately another stile right, to continue in another field with a hedge now on the right, following the electricity cables. At the far end of this field the obvious continuation seems to be in the corner beneath overhanging bushes, but this is wrong. Go a few metres left along the hedge and a stile (an iron bar) will be seen sheltered beneath bushes. There is no obvious path in the field beyond, but we descend towards the spreading, dormered, tiled roof of a seventeenth-century cottage and find a kissing-gate beneath the shades of some fine tall trees. It leads on to a surfaced road, on which we turn left to a junction, and then right.

We are in the pretty little village of Litlington. It has a pub called the Plough and Harrow, an excellent general shop, and a tea-garden.

We follow the road north through the village to the church, a small, much restored flint building, with two Norman windows to demonstrate its antiquity. Beyond the church a path appears beside the road, and we follow this past three houses called 'ham' — the Ham, Wold Ham, and North Ham — and then enter a field over an iron stile. Pass through this field to another stile a few metres left of the far corner. Here we maintain direction, crossing an obvious cart track towards a white sign in a dip. The dip contains a small pond.

 We cross a stile to pass beside the pond through a wilderness of

Westdean church

weeds and beside the boles of felled elm trees, to find ourselves on a road at Plonk Barn.

Travellers coming from Alfriston will have to look carefully for this turning off the road. There is a South Downs Way plinth, but it may be partly hidden.

Plonk Barn (which perhaps ought to contain wine!) is a flint and brick building of no particular interest except that this is the point where the South Downs Way footpath and the South Downs Way bridleway meet, to continue together across the Cuckmere into Alfriston.

Beside Plonk Barn a signpost indicates a path to Lullington church, ¾ kilometre away. The church, 5 metres square, is sometimes said to be the smallest parish church in England; it is in fact the chancel of a church the nave of which has disappeared. It has thirteenth-century windows cut in clunch (hard chalk), but the walls may be older.

Eastbourne to Alfriston (bridleway)

Distance 13 kilometres

Walkers may reach the beginning of the bridleway by taking a No. 5 or No. 6 Corporation bus from Gildredge Road opposite Eastbourne railway station to Meads; get off at Carlisle Road. Ascend this road, crossing the openings of Gaudick Road and Denton Road, bear right into Paradise Drive, pass the turning to Links Road, and you will find the beginning of the Way on the left. Kerbside parking in Carlisle Road.

Eastbourne to Jevington

Distance 6½ kilometres

The bridleway begins as a chalk track marked by a South Downs Way plinth and a bridleway plinth. (A map board here shows the route). It rises through grass and among bushes to Paradise Wood on the right. An inviting path enters the wood, but this is not our way; the wood conceals a covered reservoir, the dome of which is glimpsed. We keep the wood on our right and come to a division of tracks, with three indicator plinths; we follow that to the right, pointing to Willingdon and Jevington. Within a few metres Paradise Wood ends.

As we ascend we come to a point where the track divides into three; we keep to the right-hand track. Off to the right of this, almost hidden in the grass, is a piece of rough flint wall. It is the remains of a windmill. From the summit of the down there is an extensive view over Eastbourne and to the sea. When there is a mist the hazy water seems to extend inland over the Crumbles and the Pevensey Levels. The Way continues as a broad grassy track over downs interspersed with scattered clumps of thorn bushes and gorse, with stands of purple thistle and rosebay willowherb. This is excellent riding country.

We come to and cross a main road, with the new Downs Golf Clubhouse on our right and the golf course ahead. The former clubhouse is now the Beachy Head Youth Hostel (marked 'Club House' on the 1:25,000 map and 'CH' on the 15:50,000). We follow the wide concrete track across the golf course. When this track curves off to the left, signed to Eastdean, we continue ahead on a firm chalk surface to the end of the golf course, where a wire fence appears on our left and furze bushes appear on the right. The track is now rough and rutted. A concrete water trough on the right marks a dew-pond with a bottom of concrete. Ahead is Willingdon Hill, with a large

The Way — leaving the church at Jevington

round barrow exactly on the horizon, to the left of the track. There are several tracks running more or less parallel. We keep to the one on the left, following the wire fence. To the north is Combe Hill, which bears the remains of barrows and a neolithic causewayed camp.

We come to a major crossing of tracks. That to the south goes to Friston, that to the north to Willingdon, over Babylon track above Babylon Down. The crossing is marked by large carved stones of antique appearance, acting as signposts; they were part of Barclays Bank in Eastbourne.

From the crossing there are two tracks, a stony one and a lower and grassier one. Follow either — they join lower down. The track enters a deep wooded lane, between bushes of elder, hazel, etc., looped over by ivy and travellers' joy. The sunken lane drops down to the village of Jevington near a restaurant called the Hungry Monk — a real restaurant, not a café, and not for casual, light refreshment. Jevington has no shop, but it has a pub, the Eight Bells, ¾ kilometre up the hill.

Jevington, the 'tun of Geofa's people', is of Saxon foundation. It seems never to have grown much and is still small, but it is a pleasant little place, in a dry valley. It has a car park south of the Hungry Monk, and it has a good church.

We turn right from the junction of the lane with the village and in a few metres turn left into Church Lane, which has a South Downs Way sign. The church is twelfth-century Norman work, somewhat masked by the efforts of a restorer who was let loose on it in 1873; he radically altered the tower. Note the curious iron anchor crosses on the roof, the ship grave in the churchyard with a bronze model of a frigate (which in this age needs protection), and in the south-east corner a tapsell or pintle gate, a not infrequent feature of Sussex churches, but this one is unusual in having a stile incorporated.

Jevington to Alfriston

Distance 6½ kilometres

Car park at Jevington.

The Way goes ahead, passing the main churchyard entrance, into a path enclosed by wooden fences with trees and bushes on one side; in the adjoining fields you may see racehorses and on the right you may catch a glimpse of Jevington Place, an old house with Georgianised windows. Among the bordering bushes are hazel, maple, hawthorn, sloe, and spindle tree, and at their feet I found goatsbeard.

The path climbs under horse-chestnut trees in a wood, and comes to a junction with a wider path facing rolling cornfields. A South Downs Way plinth indicates that we turn left on the wide path and climb again beneath trees, steeply, until we come out of the wood and find ourselves at a crossing of tracks. Another South Downs Way plinth indicates that we turn to the right.

We are in a lane with a wire fence on the left and on the right groves of bushes made dense by creepers, and enlivened by yellow gorse and stands of rosebay willowherb. We pass through two bridle-gates and come out on to open land where there is a broad track going straight ahead along the top of the field, clearly an old track, and in fact this will lead you adequately. Eventually it passes the head of the impressive hollow of Deep Dean, which, according to the map, is 'Tenantry Ground'. To the south, beyond the rolling downs and the wooded hills of Litlington, the shining sea makes the horizon. Northwards, on Folkington Hill, is a derelict farm.

Eastbound travellers will find above Deep Dean a junction of tracks with one indicated by a South Downs Way plinth. Further along this track there is another plinth indicating a turn to the left. The paths are narrow canyons through the grass with several crossings. You need to aim for the far left corner of the field. It is simpler to keep left of the first plinth and follow the main track; if you do this you have a slightly less impressive view of Deep Dean.

North of the track a gate in the fence leads to a white chalk path descending the scarp. You will not know it, but you are above the Long Man, which does not become visible until you are practically on top of it. It is set on an exceptionally steep hillside, on which is a feature marked on the map as a disused chalk pit — but it looks more like a landslip. Below, half hidden among trees, are the villages of Folkington (locally pronounced 'Fo'ington') and Wilmington. Folkington, withdrawn at the end of its cul-de-sac, has a pretty little thirteenth-century church with Georgian box pews. Wilmington has the remains, mostly fourteenth-century, of a small Benedictine priory, and a church dating from the twelfth century. There is also the view of the Long Man, 73 metres high, standing with a staff in each hand. The outline was re-marked with white bricks in 1874 and cleared in 1975.

North-west, on Wilmington Hill, is Hunters' Burgh, a neolithic long barrow (note that 'barrow' and 'burgh' are from the same Saxon origin).

Thatching at Wilmington

From the gate above the Long Man the South Downs Way makes a southerly loop round the furzy summit of Windover Hill, on which there are both a round barrow and a neolithic long barrow. The views are magnificent, over the woods and fields of the Weald to the north, eastwards to the hills above Jevington, and, west and south, of the Cuckmere valley, including Alfriston, our next stop. Everywhere corn grows on the hills, except on the summit of Windover Hill itself, which spreads uncultivated flanks down to the margins of the corn.

The path descending the hill to the west is broad and white. It passes a covered reservoir — which contrasts with the great sheet of open water of the Arlington reservoir to the north – down to the crossing of the surfaced Wilmington to Litlington road, where there is room to park several cars or horse-boxes. Beyond the road the track drops down through a sunken tree-shaded lane for 1¼ kilometres to another road also leading to Litlington. Here we turn left and go along the tree-lined road to Plonk Barn, where we join the South Downs Way footpath coming from Exceat. In front of the barn we turn right (South Downs Way plinth) and descend to cross a small bridge over a narrow stream. A little farther on there is the longer, characterful timber bridge over the Cuckmere, beyond which, on the left, the spire of Alfriston church is seen above the trees. (Riders are asked to lead their horses across this bridge.) At the village end of the bridge the Way goes right, parallel with the river, for a few metres, and then left into a lane between old buildings, which leads out to the village market-place in front of the Market Inn.

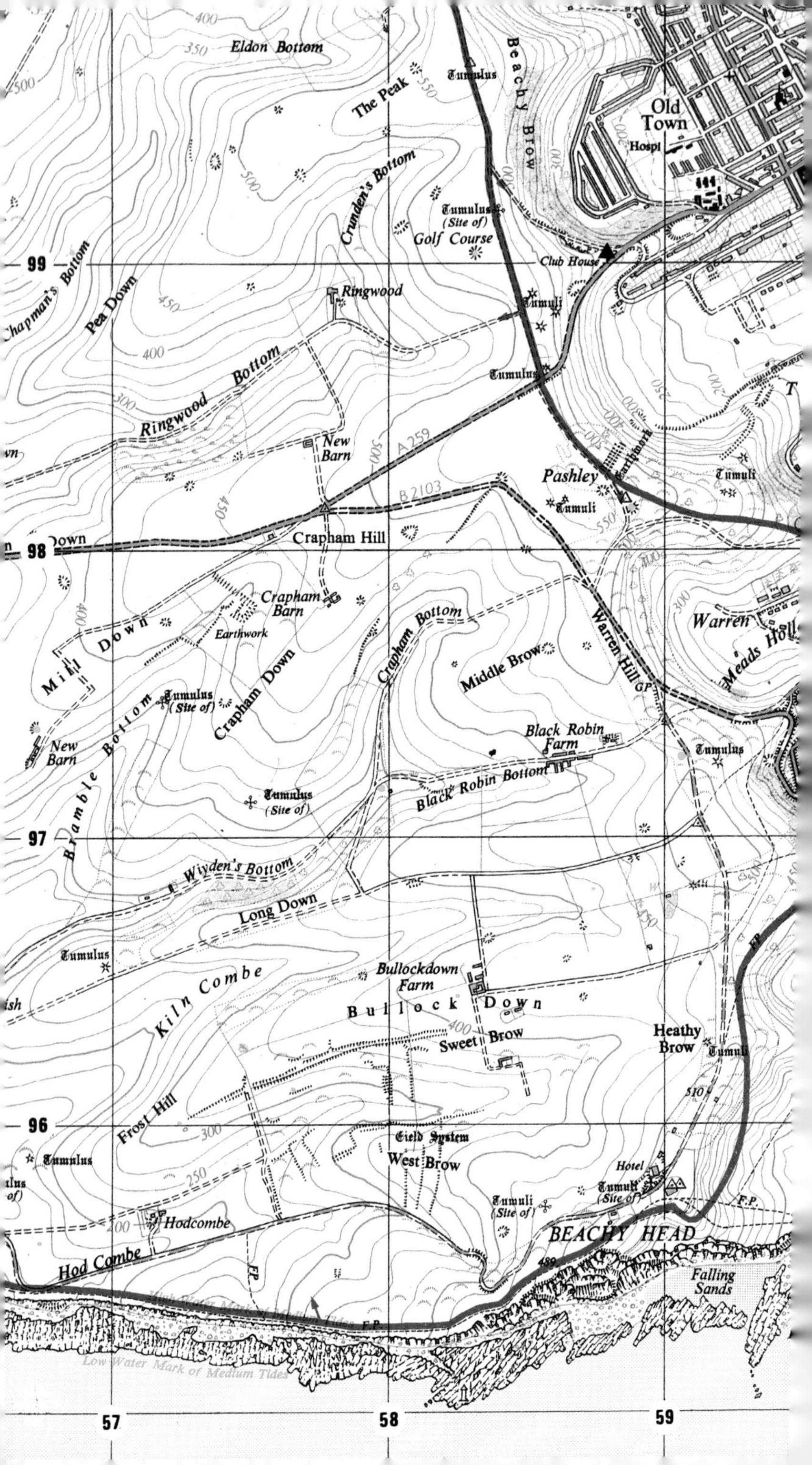

Eldon Bottom
The Peak
Tumulus
Beachy Brow
Old Town
Hospl
Crunden's Bottom
Tumulus (Site of)
Golf Course
Club House
Chapman's Bottom
Pea Down
Ringwood
Tumuli
Tumulus
Ringwood Bottom
New Barn
A 259
B 2103
Pashley
Earthwork
Tumuli
Crapham Hill
Down
Crapham Barn
Earthwork
Mill Down
Crapham Down
Crapham Bottom
Middle Brow
Warren Hill
Warren
Meads Hol
GP
Tumulus (Site of)
New Barn
Bramble Bottom
Black Robin Farm
Black Robin Bottom
Tumulus
Tumulus (Site of)
Wiyden's Bottom
Long Down
Tumulus
Kiln Combe
Bullockdown Farm
Bullock Down
Sweet Brow
Heathy Brow
Tumuli
Frost Hill
Field System
West Brow
Tumulus
Hotel
Tumuli (Site of)
Tumuli (Site of)
Hodcombe
Hod Combe
BEACHY HEAD
F.P.
Falling Sands
High Water Mark of Medium Tides
Low Water Mark of Medium Tides
99
98
97
96
57
58
59

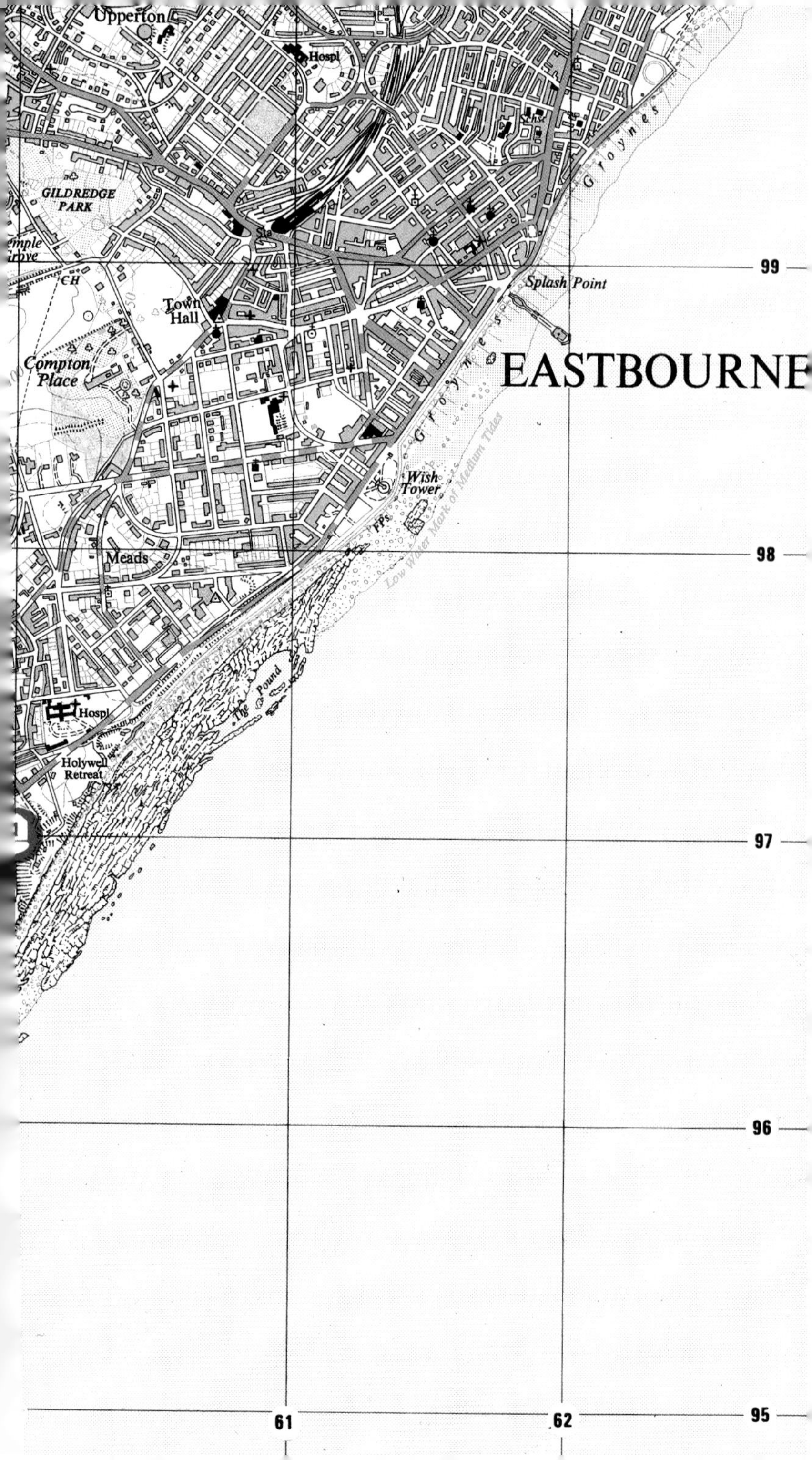
Upperton
Hospl
GILDREDGE
PARK
CH
Sta
Town
Hall
Compton
Place
Splash Point
EASTBOURNE
Groynes
Groynes
Wish
Tower
FPs
Low Water Mark of Medium Tides
Meads
The Pound
Hospl
Holywell
Retreat
99
98
97
96
95
61
62

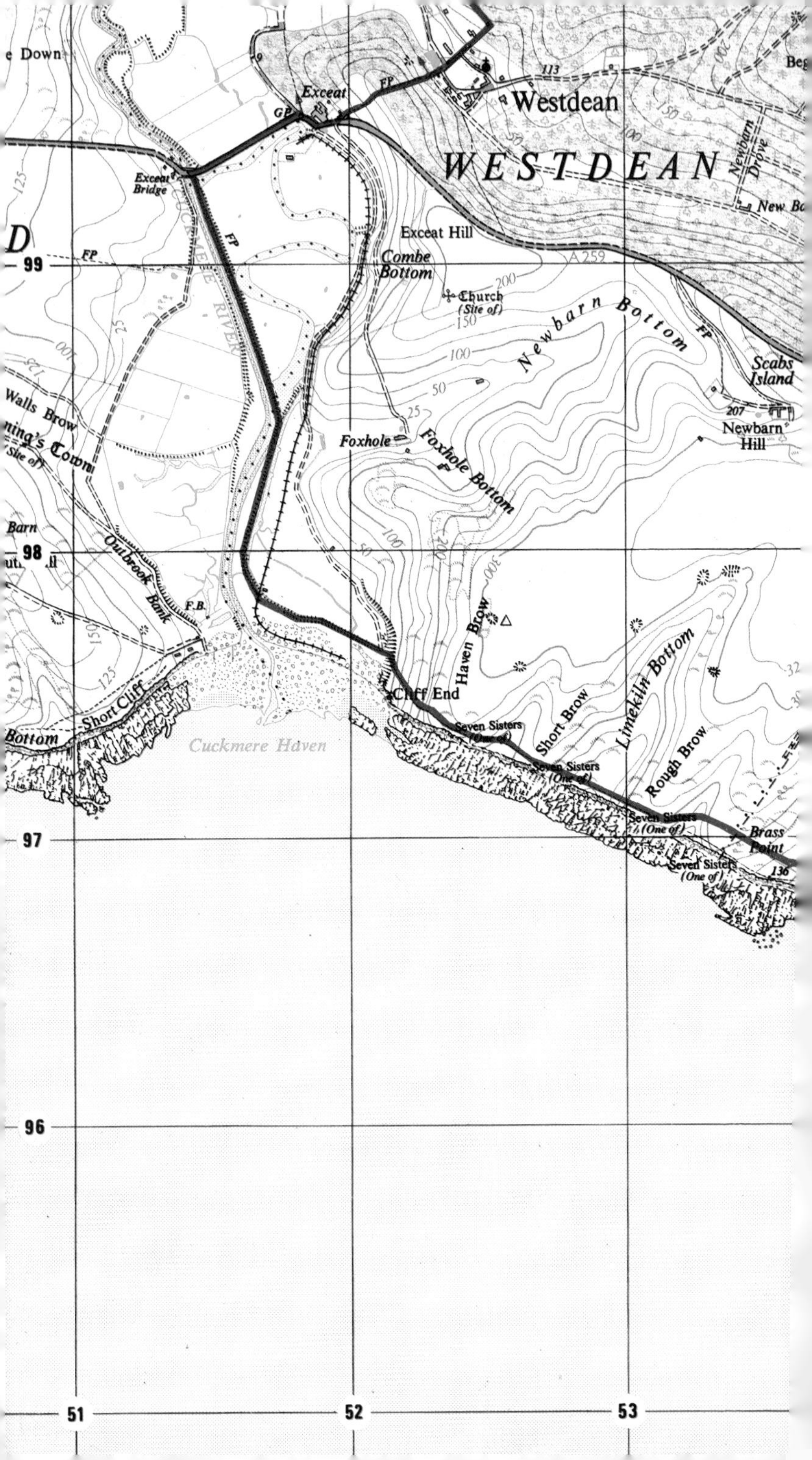

Down
Exceat
FP
GP
Westdean
113
WESTDEAN
Newbarn Drove
New Bo
Exceat Bridge
FP
CUCKMERE RIVER
Exceat Hill
A 259
99
FP
Combe Bottom
Church (Site of)
200
150
100
50
25
Newbarn Bottom
FP
Scabs Island
207
Newbarn Hill
Walls Brow
Foxhole
Foxhole Bottom
Barn
Outbrook Bank
98
300
Haven Brow
F.B.
Short Brow
Limekiln Bottom
Cliff End
Short Cliff
Bottom
Cuckmere Haven
Seven Sisters (One of)
Seven Sisters (One of)
Rough Brow
Seven Sisters (One of)
Brass Point
Seven Sisters (One of)
136
97
96
51
52
53

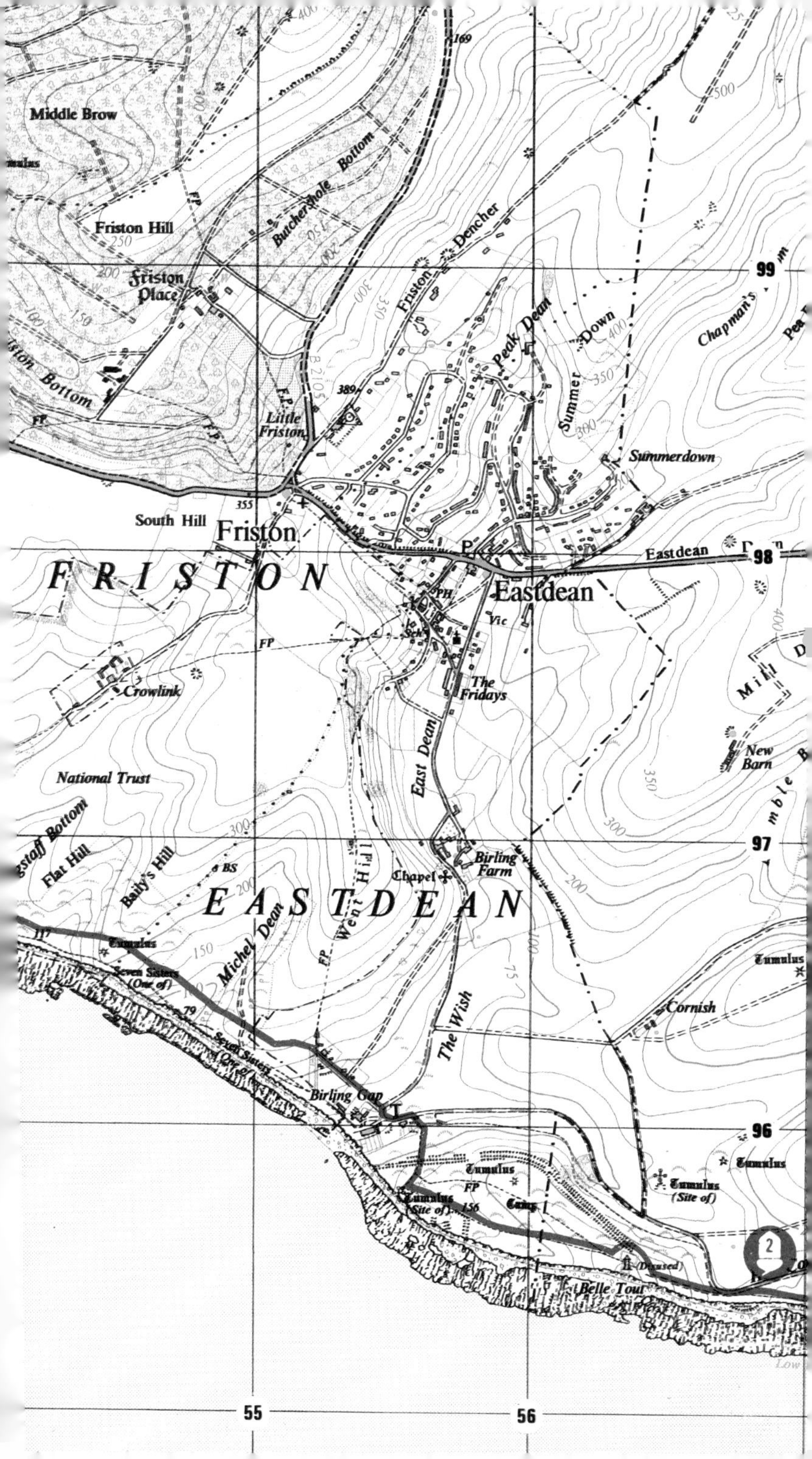

Middle Brow
Friston Hill
Butchershole Bottom
Friston Place
Friston Bottom
Little Friston
Friston Dencher
Peak Dean
Summer Down
Summerdown
South Hill
Friston
FRISTON
Eastdean
Eastdean Down
Chapman's
Crowlink
The Fridays
National Trust
East Dean
Mill Down
New Barn
Flat Hill
Baily's Hill
Birling Farm
Chapel
EASTDEAN
Went Hill
Michel Dean
Tumulus
Seven Sisters (One of)
The Wish
Cornish
Birling Gap
Tumulus (Site of)
Camp
Belle Tout
(Disused)
B 2105
2
99
98
97
96
55
56

Berwick Court
Burlough Castle
Milton Street
Wilmington Priory and remains of Priory
NTL
The Rookery Earthworks
PH
Milton Court Farm
Long Bridge
Wealdway
Hunters' Burgh Long Barrow
Tumulus
Wilmington Hill
214
152
The Long Man
Pit (dis)
Resr
South Downs Way
Long Barrow
Tumuli
Windover Hill
Plonk Barn
FBs
Tenantry Ground
Lullington Manor
Old Clergy House
Ewe Dean
Field System
Lullington Court
Park Bottom
Deep Dean
LULLINGTON CP
Church Fa
Litlington
Oldkiln Bottom
Cross Dyke
The Coombe
Lullington Heath National Nature Reserve
Fore Down
Clapham House
Clay Bottom
Chamber's Court
Clapham Barn
LITLINGTON CP
Charleston Manor
Co Const Bdy
Friston Forest
Long Brow
Snap Hill
Charleston Bottom
FRISTON FOREST
Beggar's Croft
Westdean
Middle Brow
04
03
02
01
00
53
54
3

Wood
Folkington Manor Farm
The Stud Farm
The Rough
Recn Gd
The Links
Folkington Manor
Folkington Road
Wannock Coppice
04
Wealdway
Folkington
Sch
Wannock
Reservoir
71
Middle Brow
Cranedown Bottom
Weir
Crane Down
Field System
Resr
Pits (dis)
Ash
03
Willingdon Links
Cemy
Tumulus
Filching Manor
Hanging Hill
Filching Quarry
Dean Wood
Teddard's Bottom
Jevington Road
CP Bdy
Pit (dis)
Hayward's Bottom
BSs
The Combe
JEVINGTON CP
Tumulus
Tumuli
Tas Combe
193
Butt's Brow
Helling Down
Mast
Holt Bottom
BSs
Neolithic Camp
Combe Hill
Tumulus
Butts Lane
02
Cold Crouch
Home Bottom
Wealdway
BSs
Co Const Bdy
Street Farm
PH
Willingdon Bottom
Babylon Down
Tumulus
Jevington
Field System
Tumulus
South Downs Way
Wealdway
Bourne Hill
01
Tumulus
201
Harewick Bottom
Oxendean
Oxen Dean
Tumuli
Foxholes Brow
Duttle's Brow
Tumuli
184
Willingdon Hill
South Downs Way (Wealdway)
Fox Holes
Duttle's Bottom
Tumuli
00
Eldon Bottom
56
57
58
3

Alfriston to Southease

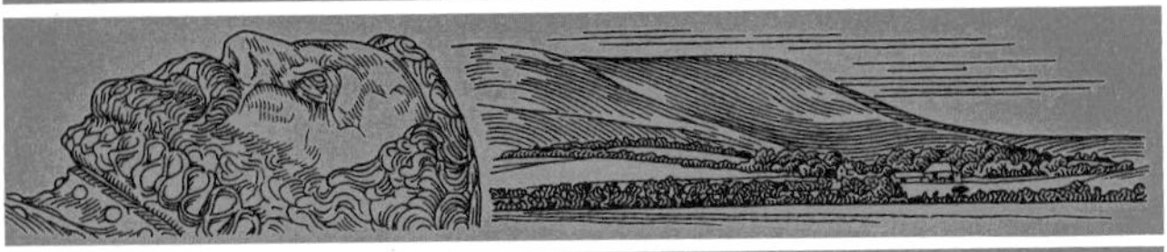

Distance $11\frac{1}{4}$ kilometres

Car park at Alfriston.

Youth Hostel in an old flint house at Frog Firle, $1\frac{1}{2}$ kilometres south.

Alfriston is one of the most charming villages in Sussex, with many pleasant old houses in its streets. In the market-place is the village cross with a hat-like stone on top of the shaft. Facing it is the Old Market Inn, also called the Smugglers' Inne — Alfriston was long a centre of smuggling. The inn exhibits a notice asking for hiking-boots and packs to be left outside. Along the street is the fifteenth-century timbered Star Inn with a number of carvings on the front, including St. George attacking the dragon with a long lance or longsword. On the corner of the inn is a ship's figurehead, a ferocious lion painted red; it belonged to a Dutch warship that fought at Southwold Bay in 1672. As a property of Battle Abbey the Star had rights of sanctuary.

Opposite is the equally picturesque, timbered George Inn, now a restaurant. Down by the church is the Clergy House, the first property of the National Trust, bought in 1896; timber-framed and thatched, it was built about 1350 and was the priest's house.

Alfriston church, known as the 'cathedral of the downs', is remarkable as having been built about the middle of the fourteenth

The George Inn, Alfriston

century and not seriously altered since. It is a noble cruciform church of knapped flint and greensand stone, standing on a mound beside the green called the Tye.

The South Downs Way proceeds from the market-place along the street and turns right round the fierce red lion.

Travellers going east should turn left along the front of the Star, and then right into the signed lane near the market cross.

Behind the Star we cross a road into King's Ride (signed South Downs Way), a street of prosperous, modern, middle-class houses. We climb this street and where it bears to the right go straight ahead up a broad and stony white track rising between bushes. We follow this up the hill, ignoring side tracks, to where it curves right, with a long view ahead. There is also a long and beautiful view back over Alfriston to Windover Hill. The track, now furrowed but very wide, rises to the site of a long barrow called Long Burgh, where several tracks meet and there is a five-armed signpost together with a South Downs Way plinth indicating both directions. A track to the north goes down to Berwick, which has a church dating from the twelfth century decorated with remarkable modern murals by Duncan Grant and Vanessa and Quentin Bell.

We now follow along the margins of cornfields, gradually rising, until we come to two gates in a fence. One is a bridle-gate for riders and the other a kissing-gate for pedestrians, a tight squeeze even for those without packs on their backs. To have two gates like this is reminiscent of the man who made two holes in his door, one for the big cat and one for the small cat! Beyond the gates is a pasture with the track showing faintly in the grass, straight ahead. It passes two round barrows, one very low and the other scarcely visible, both robbed. Farther on, where the down breaks away on the left to a sinuous valley, which is Jerry's Bottom, there is a more obvious barrow. A broad gravel path climbs Bostal Hill — 'bostal' is an old Sussex name for a hill path — passing New Pond, a dew-pond, beyond which is another barrow, a couple of metres high, with the usual hole in the middle. There are wide-spreading views of the misty distances of the Weald from the embankments of the barrow and the dew-pond. North-west, Firle Beacon thrusts its nose out above the valley and contrives to look formidable.

Beyond the barrow the top of a chalk quarry shows in the scarp and near this is an official car park and picnic place, served by a surfaced road coming up from the A27 by way of Bopeep, a farm. There are no good views from the car park, but there are splendid ones from the road, over the Weald and of Firle Beacon.

There is gliding from here occasionally and a building beyond the car park was used as a hangar for the gliders. We pass through two sets of gates and leave this building on our right. Our next aim is the beacon. The climb is gradual, towards the triangulation point, which can be seen for long distances. The sea is seen to our left, with the piers of Newhaven. On top of Firle Beacon is a huge barrow, in which a giant is said to rest in a silver coffin. The sharp fall down the nose of the beacon is protected by a fence, over which we look down to the woods of Firle Place and to West Firle church. Firle Place is a Tudor house modernised in 1730; it is open to the public and has a notable collection of paintings and furniture. It has been the home of the

Gage family since it was built about 1487. Brasses and monuments of the family may be seen in the church.

To the north is Glynde, with Glynde Place, an Elizabethan mansion built in 1567; one of its owners built Glynde church in 1765 in elegant Georgian style. Glyndebourne, which has been in the same family for seven centuries, is older; the famous opera-house was added in 1934.

At 217 metres Firle Beacon is one of the highest points of the downs and it marks the swing of the trend from west-to-east to south-east. South of the summit are the lynchets of a series of Celtic fields, and south-west are two tumuli called Lord's Burghs, the name perhaps a folk memory of the person buried there; compare Five Lord's Burgh south of Bostal Hill.

A tall radio mast is seen to the west of Firle Beacon: this, which we aim for, is some 5 kilometres distant on Beddingham Hill. We come to a pair of gates, a kissing-gate and a bridle-gate, again. The downs hereabout are excellent for riding and give opportunity for a gallop on turf. We come to a large car park at the head of a surfaced road coming up from the A27 and West Firle and pass through a bridle-gate into the car park — *the gate has a white acorn on the car-park side for the benefit of east-bound travellers* — and go on to the road head. Here we pass through a squeeze-stile beside a wide iron gate; the gate may be opened by riders. The Way continues as a clear gravel or stony track towards the radio mast, and passes by the base of the mast to another gate at the top of another surfaced road coming up from Little Dene and the A27. There is not much room for parking at this point. We cross the road-head and go through another gate.

The sea accompanies us distantly on our left, with the piers and cranes of Newhaven. We are above the valley of the Ouse, with reaches of the river having the appearance of lakes. A true lake or reservoir at Piddinghoe contains an island and yachts may be seen upon the water.

We pass White Lion Pond on our left. Nearly 1½ kilometres farther on we pass Red Lion Pond on our right, a dew-pond that is likely to be dry in summer. The surrounding embankment is a home of wild flowers that do not mind disturbed ground — harebells, lady's bedstraw, stemless thistles, yellow vetch, yellow toadflax, knapweed. On the embankment is a triangulation point, with interesting views towards Lewes and the isolated chalk down that includes the Caburn and Cliffe Hill.

Below us, at the foot of the downs, there is a large chalk pit — an excavation with a level floor — and a factory with a tall chimney. It produced chalk for the making of cement by the wet slurry process at the Rodmell factory, which was closed in 1975. The company, Blue Circle Cement, says that it landscapes its sites when quarrying is finished; it has a daunting task with this large hole in the ground. West of the factory the winding Ouse shines in the valley.

We come to a stile and gate and pass through to continue ahead over grass towards a large clump of furze. Here, beside this clump, the Way comes into full view of the broad, level valley of the Ouse, divided into square fields by drainage channels. This great flat area

Glynde Place

was formerly a marsh, out of which, north of us, rose two slight islands, Lower Rise and Upper Rise, in a district now called the Brooks. The name of the Ouse dates from the sixteenth or seventeenth century. The earlier name was the Midwind.

We look down the steep, grassy slope of Itford Hill to the Newhaven road, beside which is Itford Farm. Beyond the farm is the railway line with Southease Halt, and beyond that the village of Southease.

The clear line of the grassy track makes a large loop to the south to negotiate the slope of Itford Hill, descending to a rough chalk track that doubles back towards Itford Farm, above which we come to a gate.

The Way comes out on to the busy Newhaven road and turns right to Itford Farm, where we must cross the road to follow the Southease road, a turning between the farm buildings, with a South Downs Way sign.

Travellers proceeding in the other direction will find on the left of the main road a flight of steps up the bank: this is NOT the South Downs Way, which is just as well, as a horse could not negotiate the steps. Go on a little farther and turn up the white chalk lane on the left.

The road to Southease is not open to cars. There is a self-service railway barrier at Southease Halt that motorists are not allowed to use. They may reach Southease only by a long detour north through Lewes or south through Newhaven.

Trains to Lewes and to Newhaven run every hour through Southease Halt.

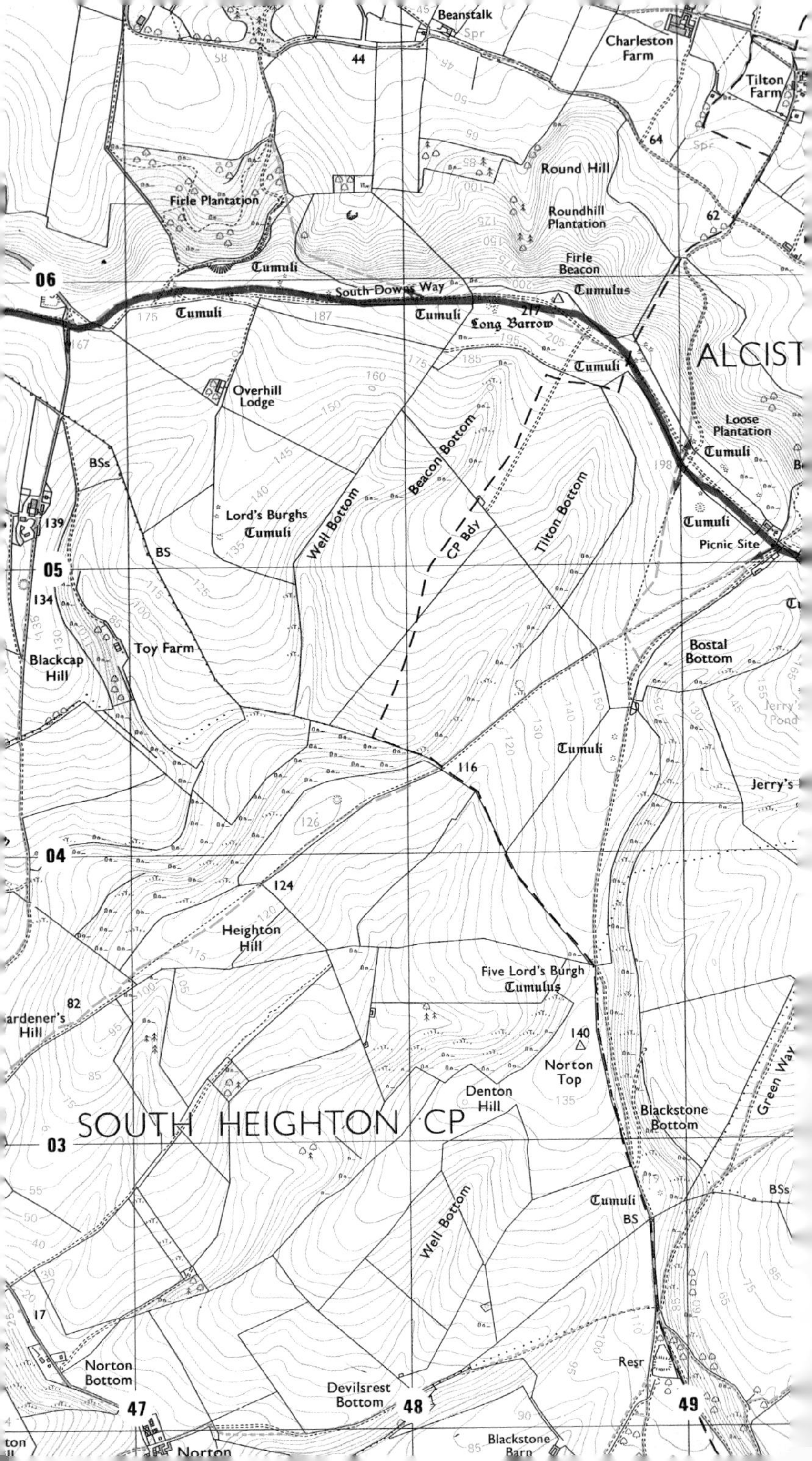
Beanstalk
Spr
Charleston Farm
Tilton Farm
Firle Plantation
Round Hill
Roundhill Plantation
Firle Beacon
Tumuli
South Downs Way
Tumulus
Long Barrow
ALCIST
Overhill Lodge
Loose Plantation
BSs
Beacon Bottom
Lord's Burghs Tumuli
Well Bottom
CP Bdy
Tilton Bottom
Picnic Site
BS
Toy Farm
Blackcap Hill
Bostal Bottom
Jerry's Pond
Heighton Hill
Five Lord's Burgh Tumulus
Norton Top
Denton Hill
SOUTH HEIGHTON CP
Blackstone Bottom
Green Way
Well Bottom
Resr
Norton Bottom
Devilsrest Bottom
Blackstone Barn
Norton
06
05
04
03
47
48
49

Carr's Barn
Selmeston House
Green House
Stonery Farm
Garage
Berwick Station
PH
PO
Mill Hill
Pol Ho
Tilton Wood
Common Lane
Weirs
Roseland Shaw
New Barn Farm
06
The Shaw
Resr
Alciston
Tithe Barn
Alciston Court
Pound Place
BERWIC
Berwick
Church Farm
Church Farm
A 27 (T)
05
Drusilla's (Zoo Park
New Barn
Tumuli
BS
Comp Barn
Berwick Court
South Downs Way
Tumuli
04
Winton Street Farm
Cross Dyke
Pit (dis)
Sanctuary
Winton
Milt
Long Bridge
Long Burgh
Long Barrow
Sch
Short Bottom
FBs
Plonk Barn
Cross
03
ALFRISTON CP
White Court
Alfriston
Hotel
Old Clergy House
Lullington Manor
France Bottom
Cross Dyke
Lullington Court
Cuckmere River
MHW
The Ham
Dukes Green
The Rails
51
52
Pingles Place
Church Farm
Frog Firle
Follers Manor

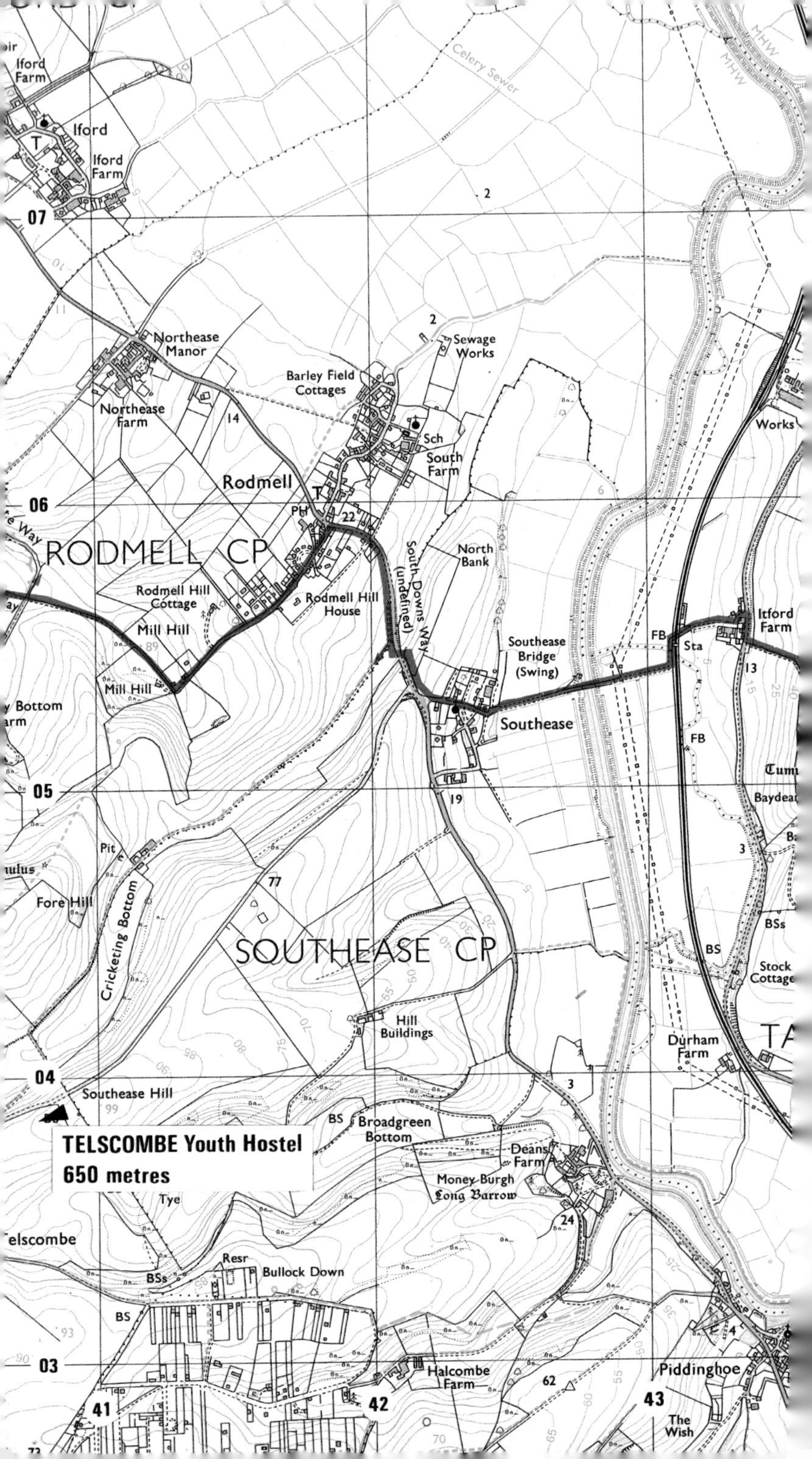

TELSCOMBE Youth Hostel
650 metres
Iford Farm
Iford
Celery Sewer
MHW
Northease Manor
Northease Farm
Barley Field Cottages
Sewage Works
Sch
South Farm
Rodmell
RODMELL CP
Rodmell Hill Cottage
Rodmell Hill House
Mill Hill
South Downs Way (undefined)
North Bank
Southease Bridge (Swing)
Southease
Itford Farm
Sta
FB
Works
Pit
Fore Hill
Cricketing Bottom
SOUTHEASE CP
Hill Buildings
Durham Farm
Stock Cottage
Southease Hill
Broadgreen Bottom
Deans Farm
Money Burgh
Long Barrow
Bullock Down
Resr
Telscombe
Halcombe Farm
Piddinghoe
The Wish
07
06
05
04
03
41
42
43

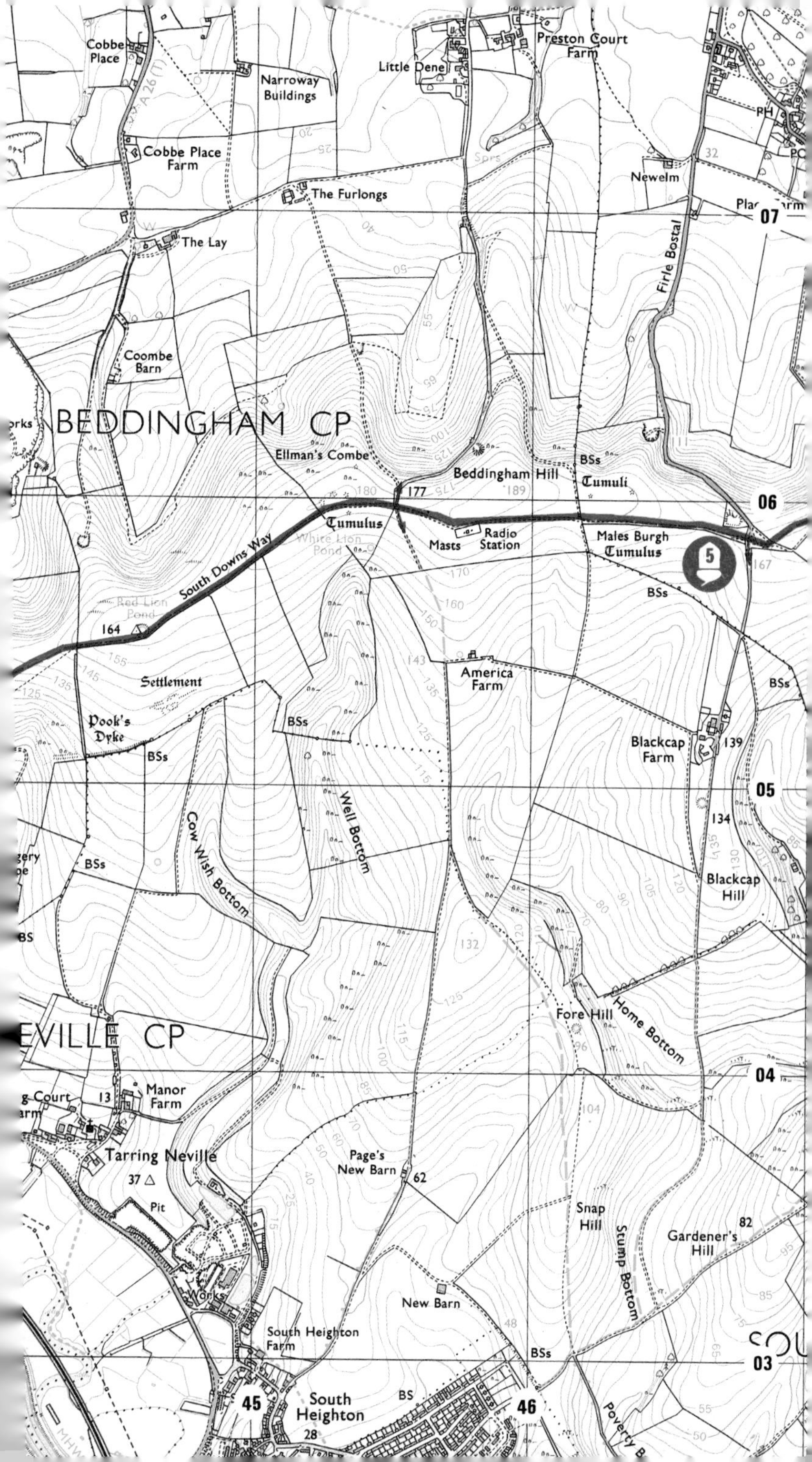

Cobbe Place
A26(T)
Narroway Buildings
Little Dene
Preston Court Farm
Cobbe Place Farm
Newelm
PH
PO
32
The Furlongs
07
The Lay
Firle Bostal
Coombe Barn
BEDDINGHAM CP
Ellman's Combe
177
Beddingham Hill
189
BSs
Tumuli
06
Tumulus
White Lion Pond
Masts
Radio Station
Males Burgh
Tumulus
5
167
South Downs Way
Red Lion Pond
164
America Farm
143
Settlement
Pook's Dyke
BSs
Blackcap Farm
139
05
134
Well Bottom
Cow Wish Bottom
Blackcap Hill
132
EVILLE CP
Fore Hill
Home Bottom
96
04
Manor Farm
13
104
Tarring Neville
37
Page's New Barn
62
Pit
Snap Hill
Stump Bottom
Gardener's Hill
82
Works
New Barn
South Heighton Farm
BSs
03
45
South Heighton
BS
46
28
Poverty B

Southease to Lewes

Distance $9\frac{1}{2}$ kilometres

The Youth Hostel at Telscombe is $3\frac{1}{2}$ kilometres south west of Southease.

From Southease Halt proceed westwards along the Southease road, crossing the bridge over the Ouse, under which the tides move rapidly. This is at a point where the valley narrows between the hills. The village of Southease gathers prettily round its green on the slope of the western hillside, the site no doubt chosen to be above flood level. The church was granted to the abbey of Hyde in Winchester by King Edgar in 996 A.D., but nothing now remains of the Saxon church. The present church is Norman. Aisles were added in the thirteenth century and later destroyed; the arcades remain. Inside are celebrated thirteenth-century wall-paintings, now all a shade of reddish brown, but with many details clear. In the jamb of the door is an intact holy water stoup, a rare survival — such things were destroyed at the Reformation; this one probably escaped attention because its unusual position concealed it. The flint tower is round, built so in order to save the cost of stone quoins, which would have been necessary if the tower were square.

We follow the road, climbing with the church on our left, and come to the junction with the A275, where a South Downs Way sign indicates that we go right. There is space to walk in single file along the verge of this busy road. The verges bear an unusual number of wild flowers of many varieties, including knapweed.

We follow the main road north for a kilometre to the Holly pub at Rodmell, opposite which we turn into Mill Lane.

It is possible for walkers only (not horse riders) to avoid the A275 by taking a longer, more pleasant footpath. Turn north from the bridge and follow the west bank of the River Ouse for $1\frac{1}{2}$ kilometres to a signstone in the bank, turn left and follow the north side of a ditch, then a track to Rodmell.

Rodmell, on the east side of the A275, has a Norman church with fine decorative detail supplemented by modern imitation Norman and Gothic; it has a palimpsest brass, i.e. a brass engraved on both sides.

Mill Lane is surfaced but narrow. At the top of the lane there is a footpath into a field, but this is not our direction. We turn right into a narrow path between fences and hedges, with a South Downs Way sign and another sign saying: 'Walkers and horses only'. It is narrow for horses, but not long. It leads to a five-barred gate, beyond which there is a small wood on the left and then more open country, with a wire fence on the right, over which there are magnificent views of the Caburn range, with the outline of the fort on the Caburn visible on the contour. The path is whitened by the daisy-like flowers of may-weed and softened underfoot by the thick foliage and the yellow buttons of its rayless cousin. Burdock too will be seen here, with spiny burrs among its large, coarse leaves. At the end of this first field is a bridle-gate and we cross a concrete track coming up from Northease Farm, and then go through another bridle-gate. A field farther on we go through a wide gate to cross another concrete track and continue straight ahead on concrete towards Front Hill. There are meadows left and right, and at the head of the meadow on the right is a ruined barrow, now just a patch of long grass and thistles.

The track passes a cattle-grid and continues with meadows on either side. We proceed along the scarp of Iford Hill and where the track swings left towards a barn on the skyline we find a placard on a post indicating a double turn for the South Downs Way — right and then left. We go through an iron farm gate beside a kissing-gate and turn left on the far side, keeping the fence on our left hand. The views over the Ouse valley are very fine. Below the scarp is the little village of Iford, which has a small Norman church, and beyond is Lewes, an ancient town with streets of fine old houses and with a Norman castle in its midst. The background to the town is the Caburn and Cliffe Hill range.

Nearer to the scarp is the grid layout of Kingston near Lewes, which not so long ago was described as a small, unspoilt village; it has expanded since then. Swanborough Manor, south east near Iford, dates in part from the twelfth century.

We follow the scarp, with its constant views, over a crossing bridleway and footpath descending to Kingston. Leaving the fence on our left we go forward to a gate in the corner of the field. Beyond the gate we head across a field towards a wire fence on the edge of the scarp and bear left to pass between two sturdy posts without fence or gate. A dew-pond is on the left among bushes. Our direction is confirmed by a South Downs Way sign. Beyond the scarp fence is a huge hollow patterned with fields. We go on through the pasture, rising to a wire fence on the horizon, along the line of the old Juggs Road, which ran from Brighton to Lewes and was said to have been used by smugglers. Ahead is a radio mast. We pass through a gate before we reach it, ignore a gate at right angles into a bridleway, and follow the fence beyond, curving to the right and away from the mast. A South Downs Way sign marks the direction.

We pass through a bridle-gate, and along the edge of a field, and then through an iron field gate, and descend past a grove of trees shaped by the prevailing wind; this is Newmarket Plantation, which is largely of beech trees, with an undergrowth of hawthorn and rowan. The Way goes down the east side of the plantation as a chalk track, and descends to pass under a railway bridge to the A27 between a filling-station and the Newmarket Inn.

There is a frequent bus service along the A27 between Falmer and Lewes, and there are railway stations at both these places.

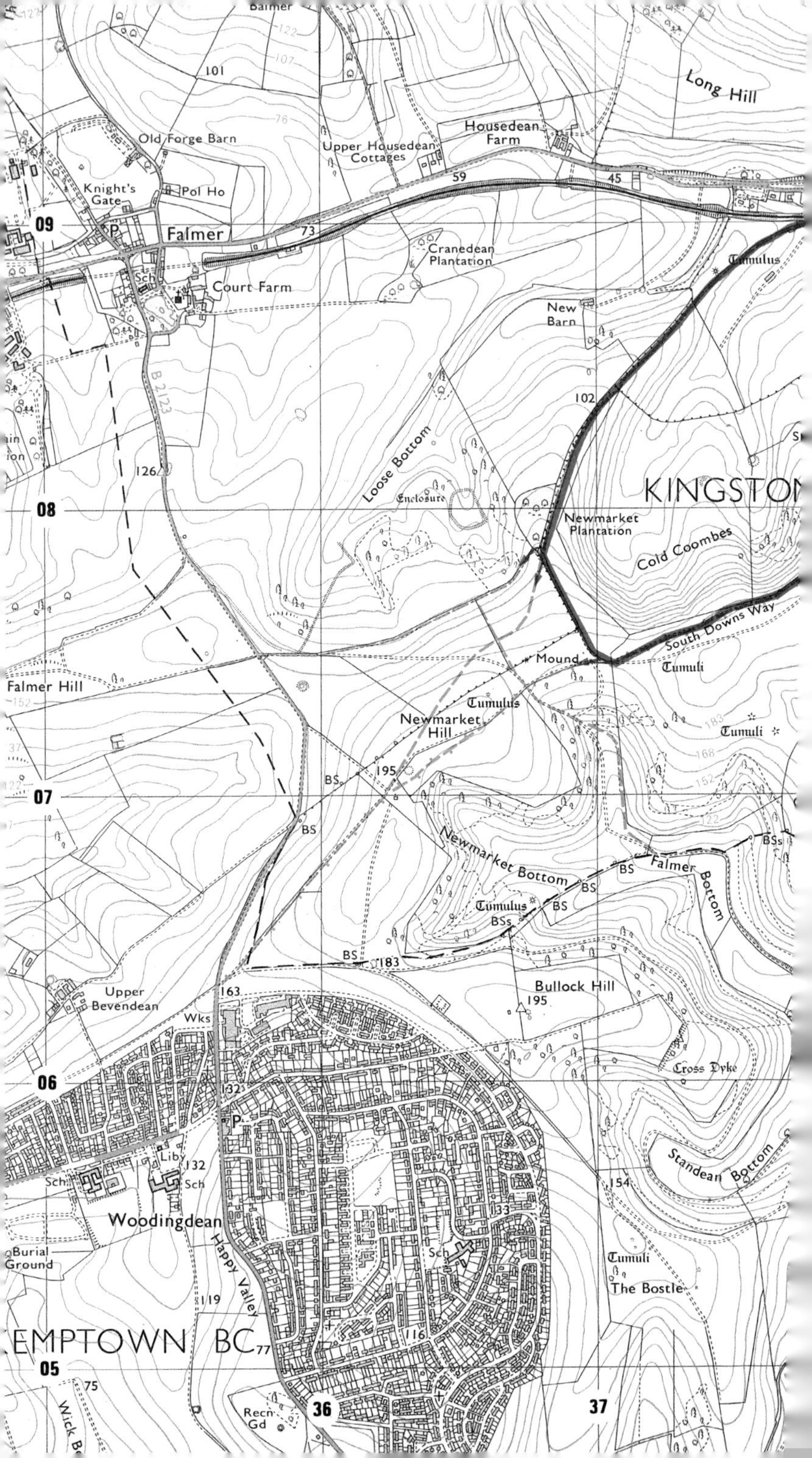

101
Long Hill
Old Forge Barn
Housedean Farm
Upper Housedean Cottages
59
45
Knight's Gate
Pol Ho
09
P
Falmer
73
Cranedean Plantation
Tumulus
Sch
Court Farm
New Barn
B 2123
102
Loose Bottom
126
KINGSTON
08
Enclosure
Newmarket Plantation
Cold Coombes
South Downs Way
Mound
Tumuli
Falmer Hill
152
Tumulus
Newmarket Hill
183
Tumuli
168
195
BS
07
152
122
Newmarket Bottom
BSs
BS
Falmer Bottom
BS
Tumulus
BSs
BS
BS
183
Upper Bevendean
163
Bullock Hill
195
Wks
Cross Dyke
06
132
P
Liby
132
Sch
Sch
Standean Bottom
154
Woodingdean
133
Happy Valley
Sch
Burial Ground
Tumuli
The Bostle
119
116
EMPTOWN BC
77
05
75
Recn Gd
36
37

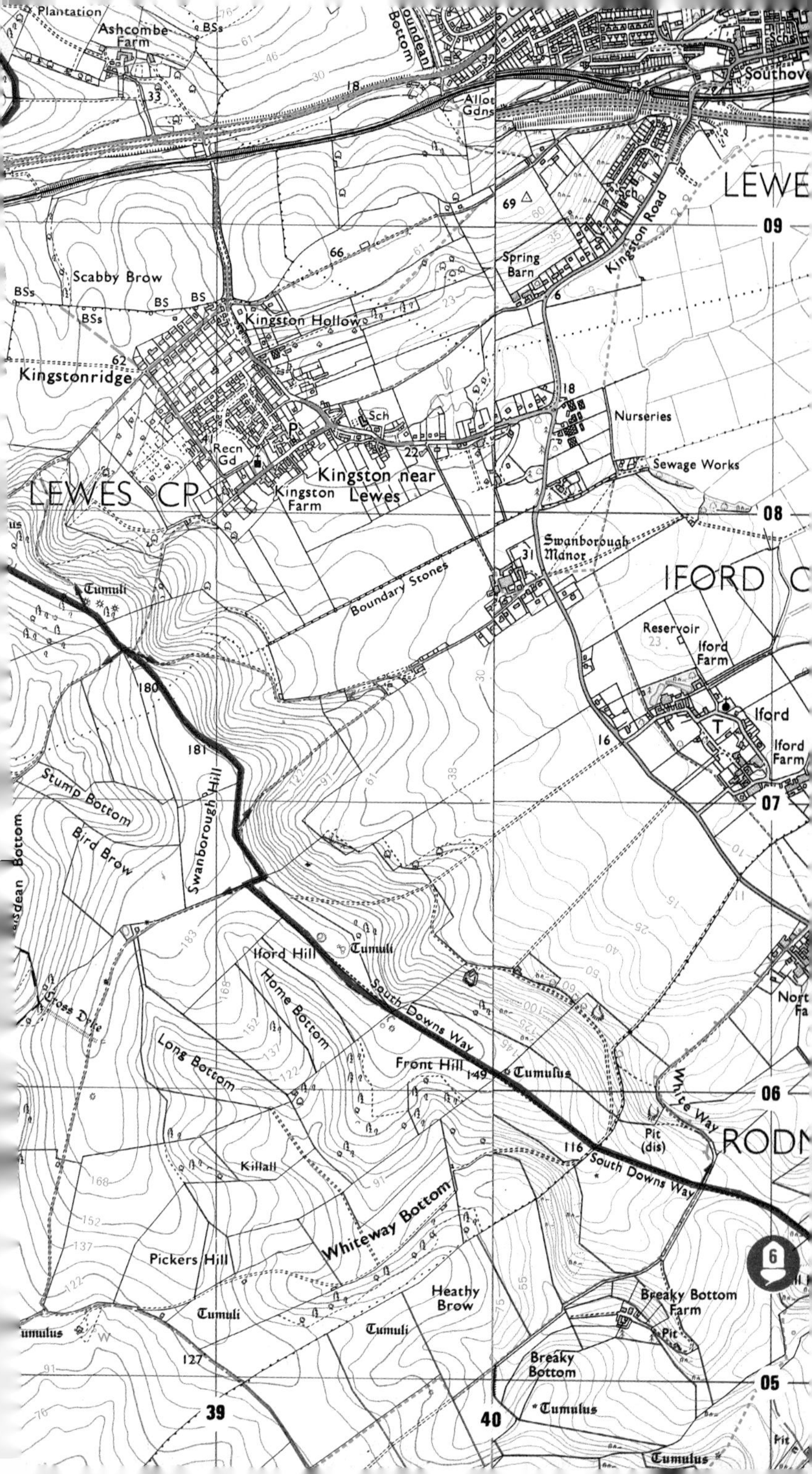
Plantation
Ashcombe Farm
BSs
Southover
Allot Gdns
LEWES
09
69
Spring Barn
Kingston Road
Scabby Brow
BSs
BS
BS
BSs
66
Kingston Hollow
62
Kingstonridge
Sch
P
18
Nurseries
41
Recn Gd
22
Sewage Works
LEWES CP
Kingston near Lewes
Kingston Farm
08
Swanborough Manor
31
IFORD
Tumuli
Boundary Stones
Reservoir
23
Iford Farm
180
Iford
T
Iford Farm
16
181
Stump Bottom
Swanborough Hill
07
Bird Brow
Bottom
Iford Hill
Tumuli
Home Bottom
Cross Dyke
South Downs Way
Long Bottom
Front Hill
149
Tumulus
White Way
06
Pit (dis)
RODM
116
South Downs Way
Killall
Whiteway Bottom
Pickers Hill
Heathy Brow
6
Breaky Bottom Farm
Tumuli
Tumuli
Pit
Tumulus
127
Breaky Bottom
05
39
Tumulus
40
Tumulus

Lewes to Pyecombe

Distance $12\frac{3}{4}$ kilometres

No obvious place for parking except a lay-by beside the A27. Newmarket Inn may be reached by bus from Lewes or Falmer.

The A27 is a dual carriageway and busy: cross with care. The beginning of this section of the South Downs Way is on the north side of the road opposite and a little east of the Newmarket Inn. It is a path running up the road embankment to a bridle-gate. Beyond the gate the path is a distinct hollow-way beside a thicket of trees and bushes. In $\frac{3}{4}$ kilometre the track swings to the right beside a wall but we go straight ahead through a bridle-gate under a large hawthorn and a fine sycamore tree. A South Downs Way signpost points the way we have come but not the way forward. We are in Ashcombe Plantation, a mixed wood through which the Way is clear as a hollow path. The ground beneath the trees is covered with ivy, among which you may find cuckoo-pint or arum lily, with a green spathe in summer or polychrome berries in autumn. At the exit from the wood there is another one-armed South Downs Way signpost.

We come into an open pasture and go straight ahead over grass, in which there are various plants of interest, including trefoils. Shortly we come in sight of a pond in a hollow and make for it. Nearby is a bridle-gate, which we pass through on to a soft carpet of rayless chamomile and speedwell. The Way follows a barbed-wire fence on the right, beside an arable field; notice how thickly the ground is scattered with flints and chips of hard chalk. The scene is enlivened by occasional plants of yellow toadflax and the yellow spikes of weld, over which fly several kinds of butterfly — fritillary, peacock, tortoise-shell, and small blue.

We come to another bridle-gate and continue beyond it with the fence now on our left. Beyond the next field the Way enters a wide lane between fences, with a concreted dew-pond on the right. The path rises gradually and passes under electricity cables to a field end and a junction of ways. The more obvious path goes to the left. We turn right on to a wide grass track towards a wood, which seems to have no name; it is on Plumpton Plain. Before we reach it we pass through a sheep pound, with a narrow alley for separating the sheep and guiding them to a weighing machine. We pass the end of the wood, which has good beech trees and pine trees, and come to a junction of bridleways. That to the east leads to Lewes, passing the site of the battle on which in 1264 Simon de Montfort defeated Henry III. The bridleway to the north descends steeply to the B2116 a little to the east of Plumpton, whose church is in the grounds of Plumpton Agricultural College. A V-shaped clump of trees was planted on the hillside above the village to celebrate Queen Victoria's Jubilee in 1887; it should have been VR, but there was not enough money for the additional letter.

Our way from the junction is west, passing a distinct barrow covered with brambles and weeds within its own wire enclosure. South of the Way were discovered the remains of the Bronze Age settlement mentioned in the introduction. It was just below the edge of the scarp, from which there is a wonderful view of the Weald. You may better enjoy this view by passing over a ladder-stile in the fence and taking a few steps into the field.

The definite track continues, wire-fenced on both sides, past Plumpton Bostal, which is surfaced as far as the Way, and on towards Ditchling Beacon. We pass Streathill Farm on our left, a lonely but prosperous-looking place with a large silo.

Ditchling Beacon, reaching 227 metres, is the third highest point of the downs. It may be reached by a road coming up from Ditchling in the north or from Brighton in the south, and this easy access makes it popular with motorists. There is ample space for parking and here in summer you are likely to find ice-cream vans and a depressing amount of litter. Below the scarp lies the village of Westmeston, with a Norman church, and beyond is Ditchling, larger and more picturesque — note especially Anne of Cleves' House opposite the church. The church is Norman and Early English.

On the beacon is a triangulation point and an indicator plaque to show the directions of elements of the broad view over the Weald. They include Crowborough Beacon 15 miles, the Caburn 5 miles, Firle Beacon 11 miles, and Chanctonbury Ring 12 miles; Blackdown 918 feet high and 27 miles distant, and the Hog's Back, above Guildford and 31 miles distant, would be visible in exceptionally clear weather.

We continue along the track running north of the triangulation point, and almost at once the motorists and casual visitors are left behind. The track is well defined. It comes to a gate, the first since

Plumpton church

Wolstonbury Hill from the Way above Pyecombe

the beacon, and soon afterwards passes a dew-pond on the left, which may be dry in summer, floored with grass, and bordered with rushes. Farther on is another pond, on the right, larger and more irregular with a rich flora of moisture-loving plants round the margin. Beside the pond we pass through an iron gate. Beyond, we cross over a bridleway, and shortly come to Keymer Post, where another bridleway crosses. Keymer Post, elegantly lettered and with an acorn finial, points to Keymer and Lower Standean, to Ditchling Beacon and to Clayton Mills. It marks the new boundary between East and West Sussex, a transition emphasised henceforth by a different kind of South Downs Way signpost and a different policy of waymarking. The height is 233 metres.

The sails of one of the Clayton windmills come into view shortly thereafter, peering above the slope of the down, with Chanctonbury Ring beyond. The windmills are slightly off the route but are worth visiting. There are two mills, known as Jack and Jill. Jill is a white timber-built post-mill, the entire upper section of which could be revolved to face the wind. Originally erected at Patcham, Brighton, in 1821, it was moved bodily across the downs, to its present position, pulled by a large team of oxen. It continued working until 1909. Jack is a brick tower-mill built in 1876. The mills are on private property. There is a car park beside them, and a road comes up to it from the A273.

Clayton village, below the scarp, has a church with a Saxon chancel and chancel arch, and an Early English nave the walls of which are covered with frescoes of the period, now mostly ochre in

colour, but regarded as important. They are true frescoes, painted on wet plaster.

The South Downs Way turns sharply south in advance of the windmills, and passes between New Barn Farm and its outbuildings. Shortly afterwards, at a crossing of bridleways, we turn right beside a golf course, which we keep on our left. Jack and Jill look down the hill at us. In $2\frac{1}{2}$ kilometres we descend to the A273. We cross this road and find on the other side a narrow bridleway running parallel with the road, behind a hedge. This comes out to the A273 again at the foot of the side-road to Pyecombe, which we ascend to Pyecombe church. 'Pyecombe' is said to mean 'gnat-infested valley'.

Pyecombe was formerly known for the manufacture of shepherds' crooks at the small smithy opposite the church. The building is now a private house displaying bellows and other tools of the smith. The churchyard gate has a shepherd's crook for its latch. The church is Norman and Early English and contains a late Norman lead font elaborately ornamented, one of the only three lead fonts in Sussex. North of the church is Wolstonbury Hill, with an Iron Age fort on the summit.

The Way goes down the road east of the church, and meets the A23 beside the Plough Garage and the Plough Inn.

Frequent buses pass the Plough, northwards to Ditchling, Hassocks, Hurstpierpoint, and Haywards Heath, southwards to Brighton. The Brighton buses pass the Patcham Youth Hostel about 3 kilometres south of the Plough.

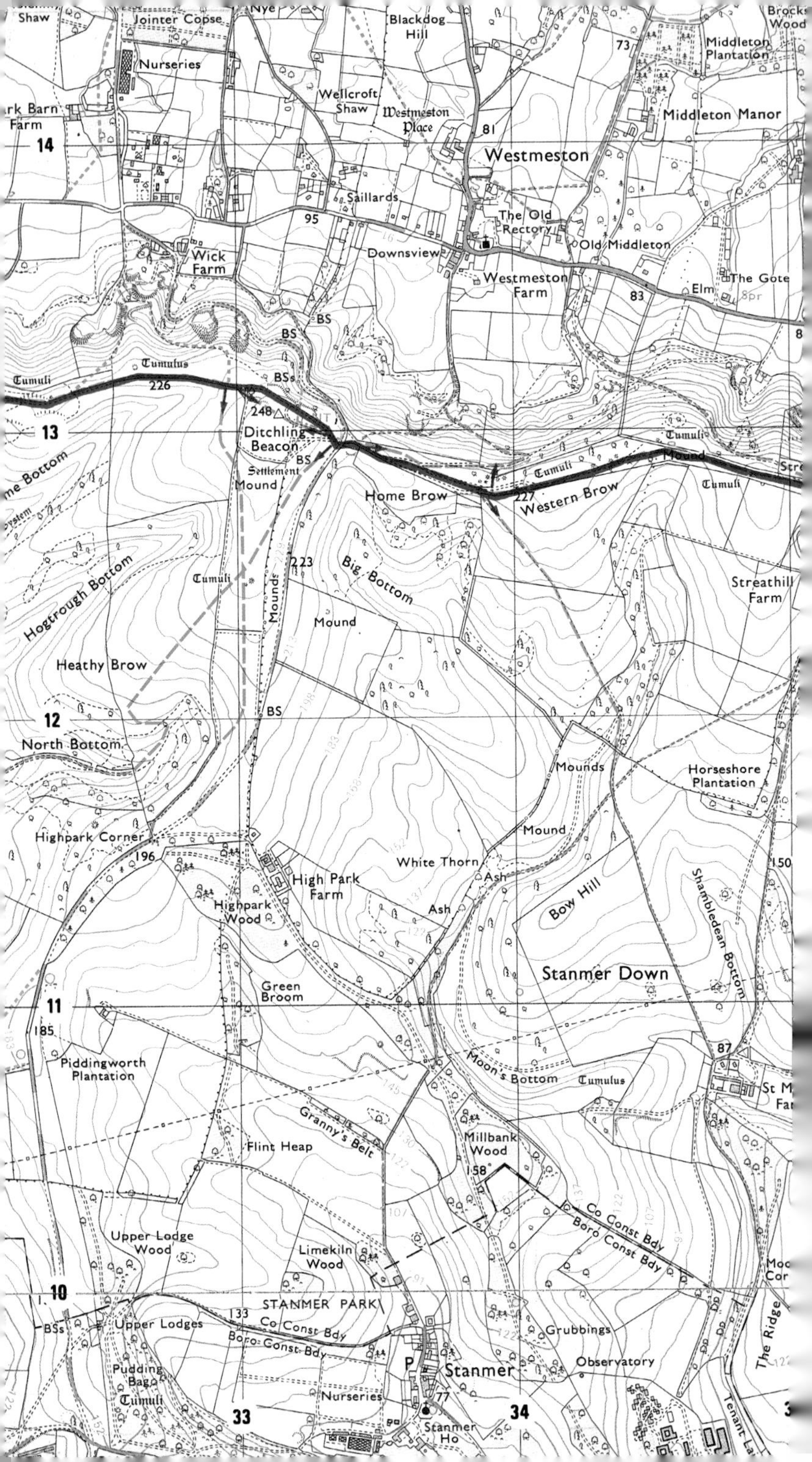
Shaw
Jointer Copse
Nye
Blackdog Hill
Brocks Wood
73
Middleton Plantation
Nurseries
Wellcroft Shaw
Westmeston Place
rk Barn Farm
Middleton Manor
81
14
Westmeston
Saillards
95
The Old Rectory
Wick Farm
Downsview
Old Middleton
Westmeston Farm
The Gote
Elm
83
BS
BS
Tumulus
BSs
Tumuli
226
248
Ditchling Beacon
13
Tumuli
Mound
BS
Settlement
Mound
me Bottom
Tumuli
Home Brow
227
Western Brow
Tumuli
223
Big Bottom
Hogtrough Bottom
Tumuli
Mounds
Streathill Farm
Mound
Heathy Brow
BS
12
North Bottom
Mounds
Horseshore Plantation
Mound
Highpark Corner
196
White Thorn
Ash
150
High Park Farm
Highpark Wood
Ash
Bow Hill
Shambledean Bottom
Stanmer Down
Green Broom
11
185
Moon's Bottom
Tumulus
87
Piddingworth Plantation
Granny's Belt
Millbank Wood
Flint Heap
158
Co Const Bdy
Boro Const Bdy
Upper Lodge Wood
Limekiln Wood
10
STANMER PARK
133
Co Const Bdy
Upper Lodges
BSs
Boro Const Bdy
Grubbings
P
Stanmer
Observatory
The Ridge
Pudding Bag
Tumuli
Nurseries
77
33
34
Stanmer Ho
Tenant La

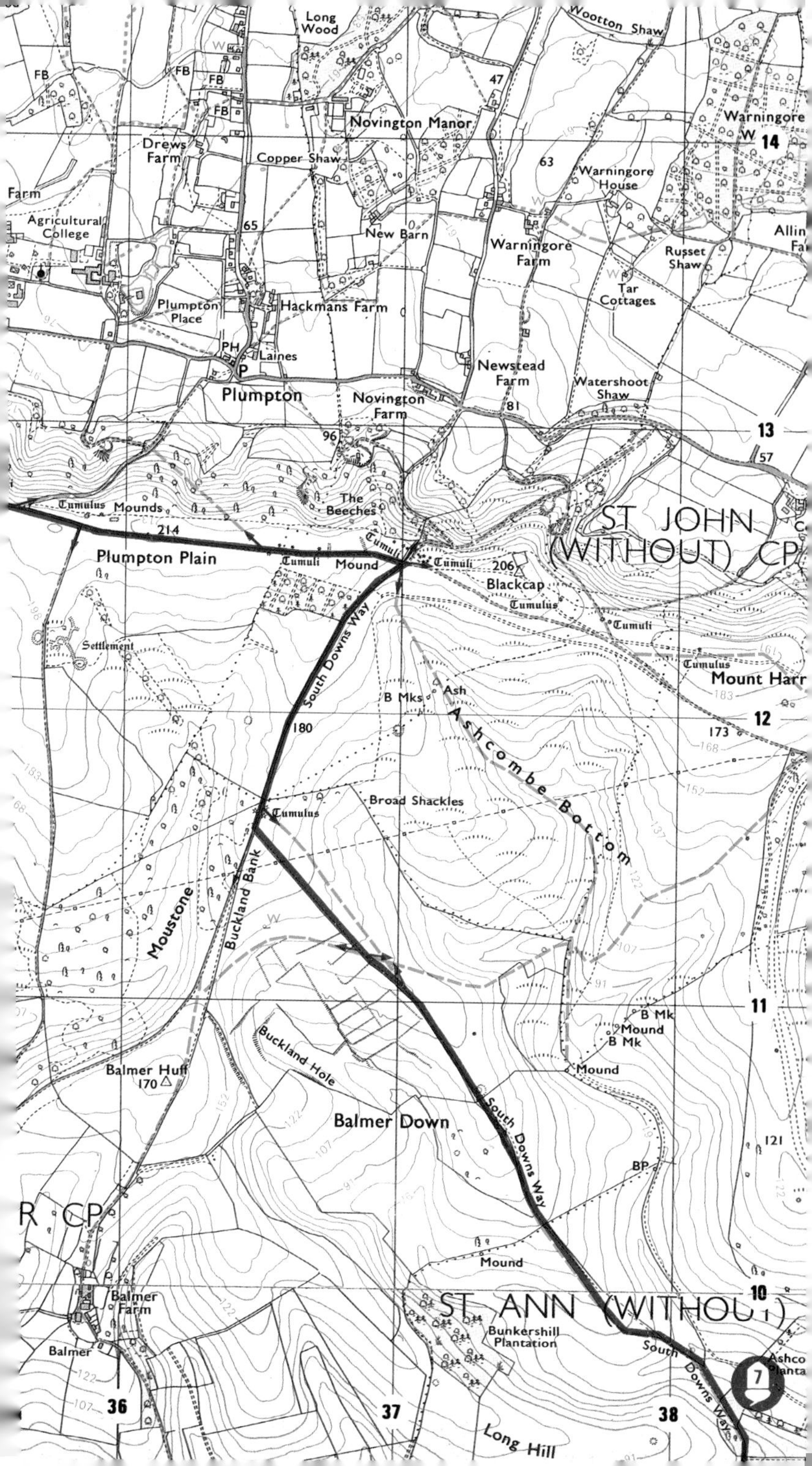
Long Wood
Wootton Shaw
FB
FB
FB
FB
47
Novington Manor
Warningore
W
14
Drews Farm
Copper Shaw
63
Warningore House
Farm
Agricultural College
65
New Barn
Warningore Farm
Allin
Russet Shaw
Tar Cottages
Plumpton Place
Hackmans Farm
PH
Laines
P
Newstead Farm
Plumpton
Novington Farm
Watershoot Shaw
81
13
96
57
Cumulus
Mounds
The Beeches
214
ST JOHN (WITHOUT) CP
Plumpton Plain
Cumuli
Cumuli
Mound
Cumuli
206
Blackcap
Cumulus
Cumuli
Settlement
Cumulus
Mount Harr
South Downs Way
B Mks
Ash
Ashcombe Bottom
183
12
180
173
168
Broad Shackles
152
Cumulus
Buckland Bank
Moustone
W
107
91
11
B Mk
Mound
B Mk
Balmer Huff
170
Buckland Hole
Mound
Balmer Down
South Downs Way
121
BP
R CP
Mound
Balmer Farm
10
ST ANN (WITHOUT)
Bunkershill Plantation
Balmer
122
107
36
37
38
South Downs Way
Long Hill
7

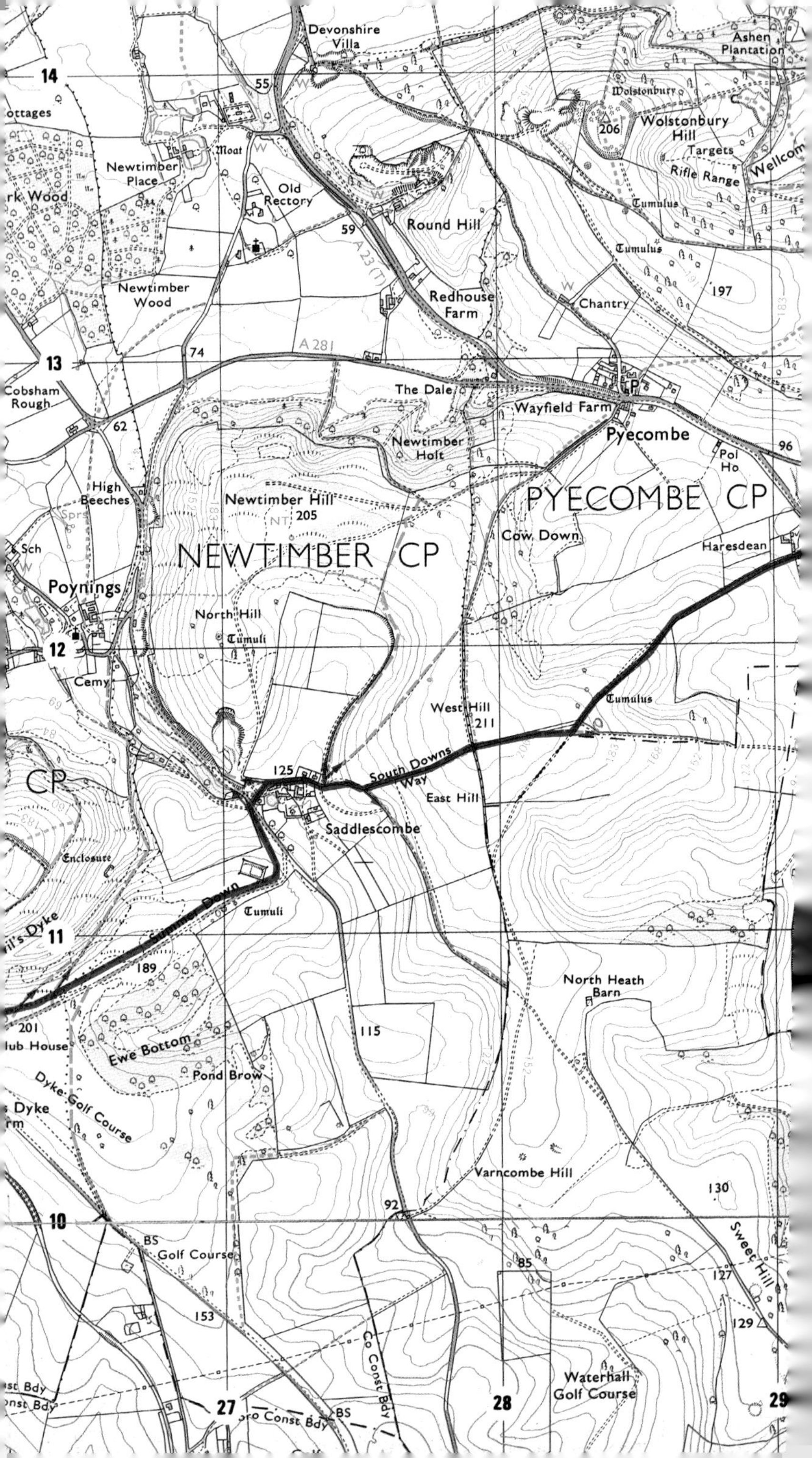
Devonshire Villa
Ashen Plantation
14
55
Wolstonbury
Wolstonbury Hill
206
Targets
Rifle Range
Wellcom
ottages
Moat
Newtimber Place
Old Rectory
rk Wood
Round Hill
59
A 23 (T)
Tumulus
Tumulus
197
Newtimber Wood
Redhouse Farm
Chantry
A 281
74
13
The Dale
Cobsham Rough
Wayfield Farm
62
Pyecombe
96
Newtimber Holt
Pol Ho
High Beeches
PYECOMBE CP
Newtimber Hill
205
NT
Cow Down
Sprs
Haresdean
Sch
NEWTIMBER CP
Poynings
North Hill
Tumuli
12
Cemy
Tumulus
West Hill
211
125
South Downs Way
East Hill
CP
Saddlescombe
Enclosure
Summer Down
Tumuli
il's Dyke
11
189
North Heath Barn
201
lub House
115
Ewe Bottom
Pond Brow
Dyke Golf Course
s Dyke
rm
Varncombe Hill
130
92
10
BS
Golf Course
85
Sweet Hill
127
153
129
Co Const Bdy
Waterhall Golf Course
st Bdy
onst Bdy
27
oro Const Bdy
BS
28
29

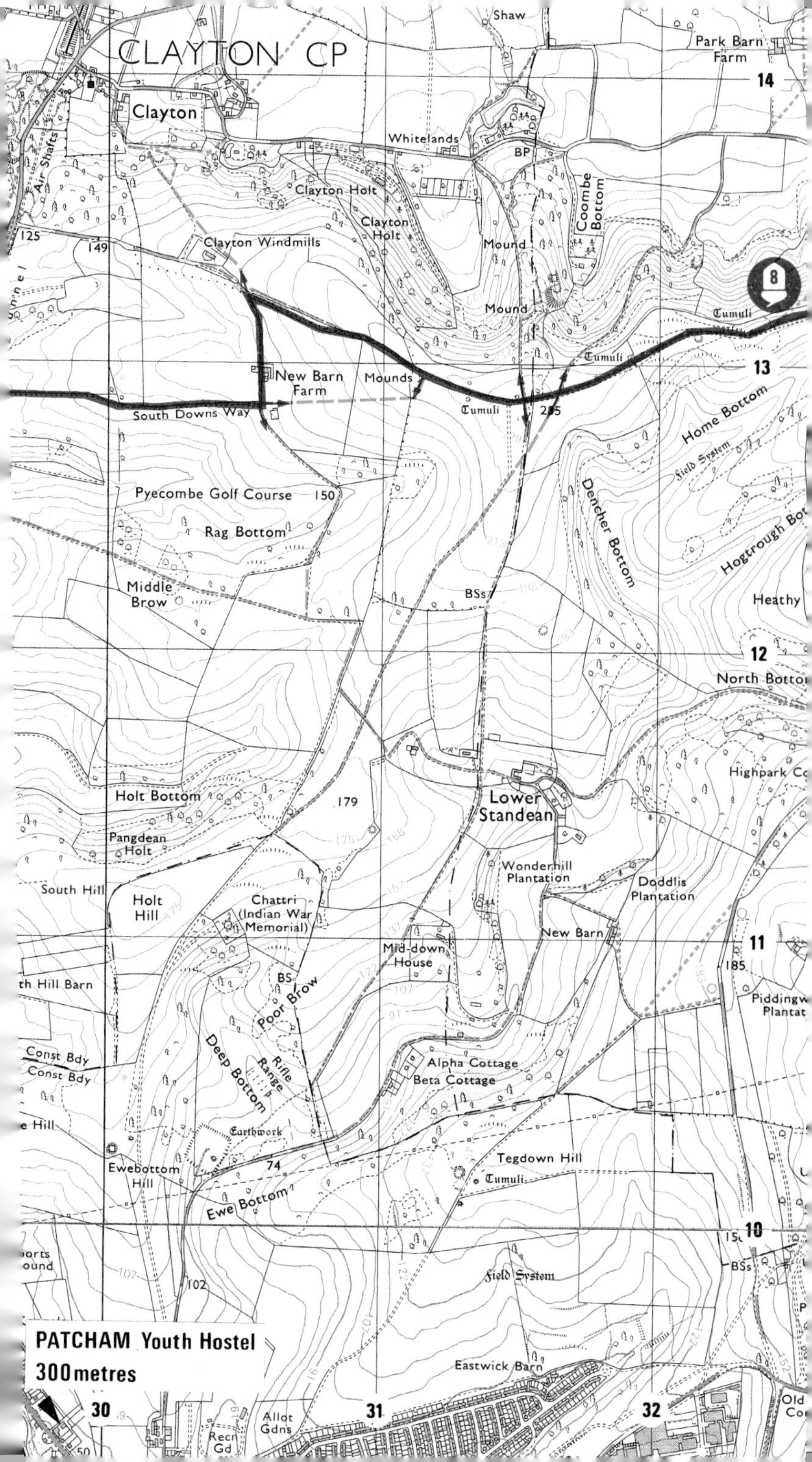
CLAYTON CP
Shaw
Park Barn Farm
14
Clayton
Air Shafts
Whitelands
BP
Clayton Holt
Clayton Holt
Coombe Bottom
125
149
Clayton Windmills
Mound
Mound
8
Tumuli
Tumuli
13
New Barn Farm
Mounds
Tumuli
205
South Downs Way
Home Bottom
Field System
Dencher Bottom
Pyecombe Golf Course
150
Rag Bottom
Hogtrough Bot
Middle Brow
BSs
Heathy
12
North Bottom
Highpark Co
Holt Bottom
179
Lower Standean
Pangdean Holt
Wonderhill Plantation
Doddlis Plantation
South Hill
Holt Hill
Chattri (Indian War Memorial)
New Barn
11
Mid-down House
185
th Hill Barn
BS
Poor Brow
Piddingw Plantat
Deep Bottom
Rifle Range
Const Bdy
Const Bdy
Alpha Cottage
Beta Cottage
e Hill
Earthwork
Tegdown Hill
Ewebottom Hill
74
Tumuli
Ewe Bottom
10
BSs
orts ound
102
Field System
PATCHAM Youth Hostel
300 metres
Eastwick Barn
30
31
32
Allot Gdns
Recn Gd
Old Co

Pyecombe to Upper Beeding

Distance 12¾ kilometres
No adequate parking.
On the west side of the A23 opposite the Plough Inn is a surfaced lane running up beside the Brendon riding-school. We follow this lane up the hill and where it bears right we go ahead through a wide iron gate on to a chalk track between widely spaced bushes, mostly hawthorn. On our right is a field with a series of jumps for the riding-school. Northwards rises the rounded hump of Wolstonbury Hill, its slopes covered with cornfields and pastures. The Iron Age fort on the summit is unusual in having its ditch within the rampart. Left of the hill there is a view over the Weald. Surveying us from their hill top to the north east are the Jack and Jill windmills.

Left of the track are hillsides covered with horizontal terraces, apparently man-made but too closely spaced to be ordinary lynchets.

Farther up the hill the track becomes several parallel tracks. Keep to the left, by the wire fence, to the top left-hand corner of the field. Beyond the gate bear off right as indicated by a South Downs Way sign into a narrow lane between wire fences. From this lane the east-bound traveller has a view of Ditchling Beacon and of Jack and Jill. To the south there is the conurbation of Brighton, Hove, Portslade, Southwick, and Shoreham, with several multi-storey blocks. Pass through two bridle-gates close together on West Hill and descend beside the fence on the left through pastures thick with ragwort. The forward view includes the Devil's Dyke and, yet more distant, Chanctonbury Ring, from the foot of which the Weald spreads far and wide to the North Downs.

We follow the fence downhill, with the roofs of the hamlet of Saddlescombe lost and found among trees below, and enter a narrow, tree-shaded sunken lane, which in wet weather will be muddy, broken up by horses' hoofs. At the foot of the lane, on the right, is a National Trust signboard for Newtimber Hill, a hill with ancient lynchets on the south and west slopes. We pass through an iron farm gate and go on through the hamlet of Saddlescombe, between cottages and barns, to find beyond the barns a South Downs Way sign pointing left. We descend a few metres to pass between a cottage and a small triangular green covered with mature trees. Here we cross a surfaced road going from Poynings down to Brighton. Poynings, locally pronounced 'Punnings', is a pleasant village with a lofty church of the fourteenth century, which may be compared with that of Alfriston. The village is only ¾ kilometre from Saddlescombe, below the scarp of the Devil's Dyke.

At Saddlescombe we cross the road and take a track opposite, going uphill beneath a large ash tree. We pass the corner of a raised reservoir surrounded by iron railings, and come upon an open and uncultivated tract of ground, with many paths, which shortly enter in among bushes. We need to keep parallel with the road that runs on our left from Saddlescombe to the Devil's Dyke. This hilltop is a popular resort of motorists and picnickers, and also a resort of litter-louts and dumpers, who leave old washing-machines and fridges, etc., beside the paths.

The Devil's Dyke is like a deep and enormous, dry and grassy moat, much bigger than you may expect, and if it were not so large you might suppose it to be man-made. Prehistoric man took advantage of its defensive possibilities by building a fort on the hill it encloses, and you may still see the ramparts. The dyke is said to have been dug by the Devil to let the sea into the Weald and drown all the Christian churches there. He was interrupted by the light of an old woman's candle, which he thought was the sunrise.

Within the fort is a modern hotel. Unless you are thirsty you do not need to go as far as the hotel. South of it we find and cross the road at a point where a South Downs Way plinth points into a field. There is

Newtimber Hill, Saddlescombe

Devil's Dyke

no visible path through this field. The ramparts of the fort are seen on the right, with a triangulation point on top of them, and ahead is Chanctonbury Ring. We cross the field, bearing left to a gate in the far left-hand corner. Southwards shows the sea, with the cranes and gantries and chimneys of Southwick and Shoreham Harbour. To the north is a vast panorama of the Weald, all its trees, and fields and villages, into the far distance and the hazy line of the North Downs; it gives an idea of the dimensions of the geological dome or anticline from which the Weald and both the North and South Downs are derived.

Beyond the gate follow the evident path towards another gate, passing an improvised stile on the right — it gives access to a footpath that passes what appear to be irregular earthworks and goes down towards Fulking, a village with several old houses and a monument to John Ruskin. We pass over Perching Hill and beneath a line of pylons, and find the rounded dome of Edburton Hill ahead. The whole hill is cornland and the Way does not go over the summit, on which, on the north side and not seen, is Castle Rings, the motte and bailey of a small Norman castle, built in this unusual position to guard the boundary between the rapes of Lewes and Bramber. We skirt the south side of the hill, following a fence. A bridleway goes down to Edburton village and another goes south to Southwick. Edburton is a pleasant village with a thirteenth- to fourteenth-century church containing a piscina chained to the floor and a Norman lead font — compare with the one at Pyecombe.

From Edburton Hill the South Downs Way is seen ahead climbing to Truleigh Hill Barn, which has a silvery silo in front of it and two radio masts near by.

Beyond Truleigh Hill Farm there is a crossing — a bridleway to the left to Southwick and a footpath north to Truleigh Manor Farm. There is also a sign for a Youth Hostel. The hostel is straight ahead, among pine trees on the right. Originally built as a summer-house on brick stilts in the 1930s, the building has been modernised and extended with the help of a grant from the Countryside Commission to become one of the Association's finest modern hostels.

Beyond the hostel we pass through a wood. Where the wood ends a sign on the right seems to point straight ahead along a surfaced road, but in fact it points to a narrow path just inside the right-hand hedge. This path runs parallel with the road for about 1½ kilometres, alongside an enormous field. It comes out through a gate to a cross-roads, where a six-armed sign erected by the Sussex Downsmen in 1973 stands beside a small car park. Chanctonbury Ring shows ahead. We follow the direction for the South Downs Way indicated by the signpost and within a few metres find another South Downs Way signpost and a bridle-gate on the left. This leads into a field in which the Way is a grassy track towards the corner of a fence ahead. We keep this fence on our right. As we descend the Adur becomes visible in the valley and Lancing College chapel stands tall against the sea.

We descend alongside an arable field, looking down towards the new bridge over the Adur, at the far end of which, among trees, is Botolphs church. North of it is Bramber, with its shattered Norman castle. The track becomes a lane and this joins the A283.

Buses run along the A283 north to Steyning and Washington and south to Shoreham by Sea.

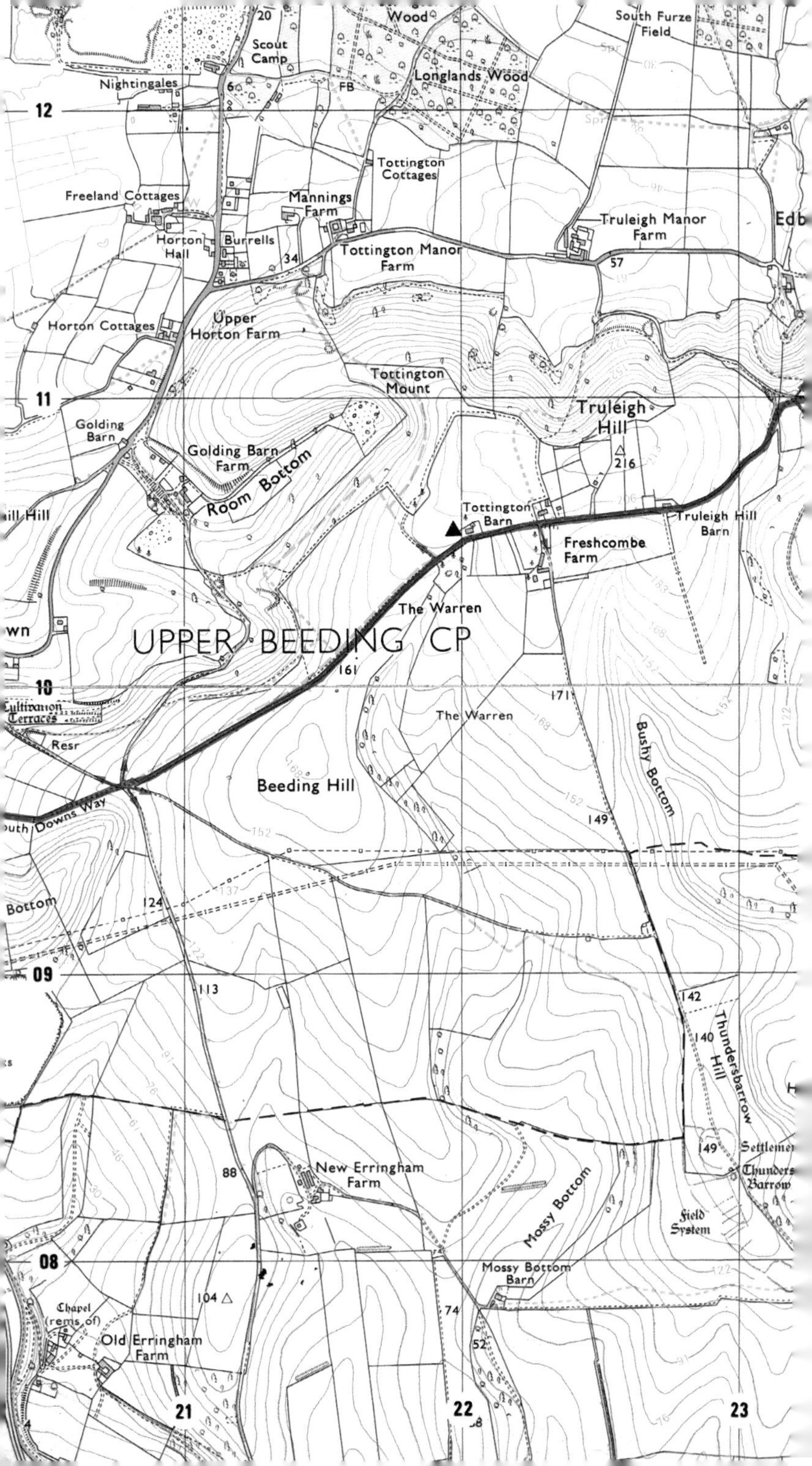
Wood
South Furze Field
Scout Camp
Nightingales
Longlands Wood
FB
12
Tottington Cottages
Freeland Cottages
Mannings Farm
Truleigh Manor Farm
Edb
Horton Hall
Burrells
Tottington Manor Farm
34
57
Upper Horton Farm
Horton Cottages
Tottington Mount
11
Truleigh Hill
Golding Barn
Golding Barn Farm
Room Bottom
216
Tottington Barn
Truleigh Hill Barn
Freshcombe Farm
The Warren
UPPER BEEDING CP
161
10
Cultivation Terraces
Resr
171
The Warren
Bushy Bottom
Beeding Hill
South Downs Way
149
Bottom
124
09
113
142
140
Thundersbarrow Hill
149
Settlement
Thundersbarrow
New Erringham Farm
88
Mossy Bottom
Field System
08
Mossy Bottom Barn
104
Chapel (rems of)
74
52
Old Erringham Farm
21
22
23

Perchingsands Cottages
FB
Hovel
thorne
arm
47
55
FULKING CP
Fulking
P
PH
63
Springs
Wd Pp
Wickhurst Barns
Wd Pp
67
POYNINGS CP
Sch
Poynings
12
Cemy
P
63
Enclosure
215
Fort
Motte & Bailey
213
Devil's Dyke Hotel
Devil's Dyke
11
177
Cumulus
217
Downs Way
Perching Hill
Fulking Hill
Masts
201
Club House
9
Adder Bottom
Devil's Dyke Farm
Dyke Golf Course
Perchinghill Barn
Co Const Bdy
Boro Const Bdy
Cumulus
167
Scabes Castle
155
10
Co Const Bdy
Mound
Field System
Co Const Bdy
Boro Const Bdy
Tenant Hill
124
Cumulus
09
113
97
Benfield Valley
Mount Zion
Cockroost Hill
Cockroost Bottom
122
66
Northlane Barn
82
Mileoak Barn
Mile Oak Farm
Resr
Benfield Hill
08
Wks
47
Mile Oak
New Barn
Foredown Hill
24
25
26

Upper Beeding to Washington

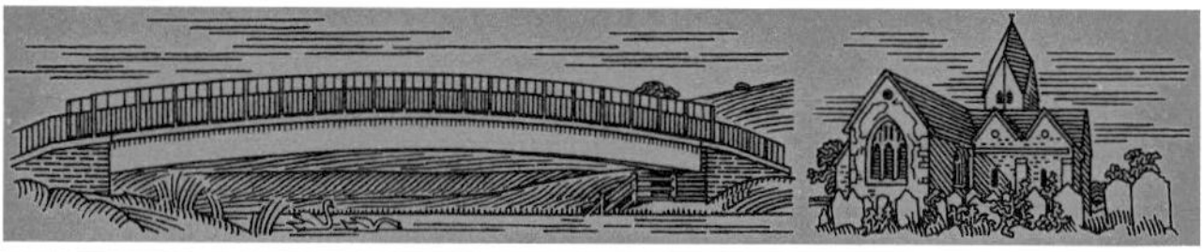

Distance $10\frac{1}{2}$ kilometres
No parking.
From the lane end where we finished the previous journey we go south down the A283 towards a large cement works. A bridle-gate on the west side gives on to a fenced path leading to the bridge over the Adur. The Adur here is a wide river between embankments. The name dates from 1613, when Michael Drayton used it in his *Polyolbion,* supposing that the Roman Portus Adurnis stood at the mouth of this river. It was previously called Bramber Water. The village of Bramber is $1\frac{1}{2}$ kilometres to the north, by footpath along the river bank. It has an interesting Norman church on the same abrupt hill as the Norman castle built of flint in 1083 by William de Braose; little more than one massive wall of the castle survived the destruction by Parliamentarians in the Civil War. St Mary's is a fine example of a medieval timber-framed house; it is open to the public.

Having crossed the bridge over the Adur, a foot and horse bridge specially built by West Sussex County Council and financed by the Countryside Commission to take the South Downs Way over the river, we turn north for a short distance on the embankment, and then away from the river to a road near the hamlet and the church of Botolphs. The site of the vanished medieval village is marked by mounds in the fields north of the road. The church is partly Saxon, with an unusual roll-moulded Saxon chancel arch supported on capitals carved as nets. The arches of the former thirteenth-century aisles show in the walls.

We follow the road northwards from the church, climbing steadily, passing the ancient Annington Farm, which has a Horsham stone roof, and Annington Manor, an old house with a Georgian front. Higher up the road turns off to the right and we take a lane to our left marked by a South Downs Way signpost. Where the lane veers left to Tinpotts Cottage we veer right to a field gate topped by barbed wire. Beyond that are some black corrugated buildings, and then another gate. Southwards the land falls to a deep hollow, which is Winding Bottom, with Coombe Head marked by a small clump of trees, where, according to the map, a Saxon spear-head was found in 1847. In the distance is the sea, which forms our horizon for many miles henceforth. We follow the fence on our left to the end of an extensive field on Annington Hill, where there is a gate and a South Downs Way signpost. Follow the path to the right; this more or less follows the field boundary and the northern edge of the field, below which is a deep hollow, Sopers Bottom, in which a white track is seen going to a farm. At the far end of the field we turn left for half a dozen steps to a bridle-gate, and beyond this continue in the same direction, with a fence on the right. The yellow spikes of weld are seen frequently along this path. Hang-gliding is practised on the steep slopes of Soper's Bottom and there is a good view from the path.

We come to a gate leading on to the road between Steyning and Sompting. Northwards the road runs over Steyning Round Hill, where in 1949 an urnfield was discovered with about thirty urns inverted over cremated bones.

Steyning (often pronounced 'Stenning'), 3 kilometres away, is a delightful little town, with many ancient houses, a picturesque clock tower, and an old grammar school. The fine Norman church has carved capitals and arches of cathedral quality.

From the gate we go along the road, passing a car park for hang-gliding enthusiasts, and where the road bears to the right we go through a gate on the left, indicated by a South Downs Way signpost, at the foot of which grow white clover, yellow toadflax, and weld. We follow the Way uphill along a good grassy headland with a fence on the left. Through another gate the Way keeps straight ahead across an enormous arable field. We pass a triangulation point on our left. The triangulation point is at a height of 189 metres above the distant sea. Clearly seen to the south are the ramparts of Cissbury Hill fort, some 3 kilometres away.

About 3 kilometres from the road the Way passes through a bridle-gate beside a cattle grid on to a wide expanse of grassland.

St. Mary's, Bramber

Steyning: Grammar school and old houses

This is crowned by the trees of Chanctonbury Ring, which have been shaped by the prevailing south-west wind. The ring is a prehistoric oval earthwork. The famous clump of trees, said to be visible 61 kilometres away, was planted by Charles Goring of Wiston House in 1760, when he was a boy. He carried bottles of water up to the ring daily to establish his seedlings. He lived to be ninety years old and to see his trees grown tall. At eighty-five he celebrated his achievement in verse:

How oft around thy Ring, sweet Hill,
A Boy, I used to play,
And form my plans to plant thy top
On some auspicious day.

The trees are mostly beeches, but there are also ash, pines, and sycamore, and not all date from 1760.

In the centre of the ring is a wired enclosure, the site of a square Romano-Celtic temple, in which were found coins and pottery dating back to the first century A.D.

Wiston House (pronounced 'Wisson') lies below the scarp, in its beautiful park. It is an altered Elizabethan house, not open to the public; it is now a European conference centre. Near the house is Wiston church, with monuments of the successive owners of the house.

Above left: Norman capital in Steyning church; above right: Steyning church; above: Chanctonbury Ring

We leave Chanctonbury Ring south-westwards across the grassy down, passing a triangulation point at 238 metres, towards a gate in a corner. Beyond this gate is a dew-pond. Its distinction is that, though not ancient — it was originally made in the 1870s — it has been restored by the Sussex Downsmen. It retained water even in the scorching summer of 1976. It also contains water-lilies, while the banks form a rich site for botanical study and discovery.

An obvious chalk path goes ahead from the gate, an ancient trackway down to North End, and we follow this for a short distance, as far as a South Downs Way signpost pointing to the right, along a rough track beside a hedge. This shortly becomes a gravelled track descending steeply, and this in turn becomes a bare chalk track deeply eroded to a V profile and descending a steep slope. This chalk track is not easy going even for a pedestrian. A horse would be better led.

At the bottom of the hill ignore crossing tracks and go ahead to bear left to the main road, the dual carriageway A24.

There are bus stops near the junction. Buses go north to Storrington, Pulborough and Horsham, and south to Worthing.

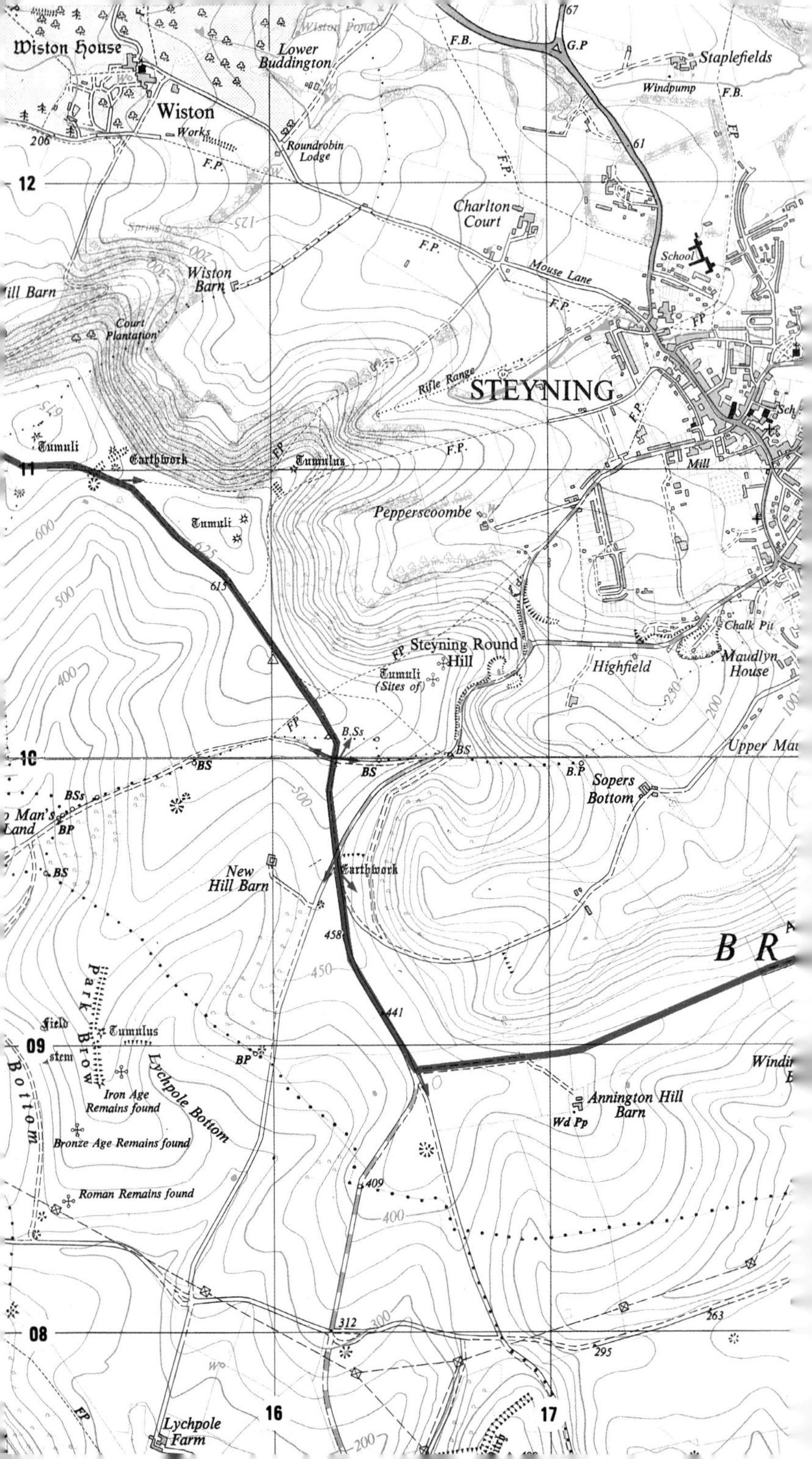
Wiston House
Wiston
Works
Lower Buddington
Wiston Pond
Roundrobin Lodge
F.B.
G.P
Staplefields
Windpump
F.B.
67
61
206
F.P.
12
Charlton Court
Spring
125
200
300
F.P.
Mouse Lane
School
Wiston Barn
Court Plantation
Rifle Range
STEYNING
F.P.
FP
Tumuli
Earthwork
Tumulus
F.P.
Mill
11
Tumuli
Pepperscoombe
600
625
615
500
Steyning Round Hill
FP
Tumuli (Sites of)
Highfield
Chalk Pit
Maudlyn House
400
250
200
100
FP
B.Ss
10
BS
BS
BS
B.P
Sopers Bottom
Upper Ma
BSs
BP
BS
500
New Hill Barn
Earthwork
458
450
B R
441
Park Brow
Field
Tumulus
09
Lychpole Bottom
BP
Iron Age Remains found
Bronze Age Remains found
Bottom
Annington Hill Barn
Wd Pp
409
400
Roman Remains found
312
300
263
295
08
16
17
FP
Lychpole Farm
200

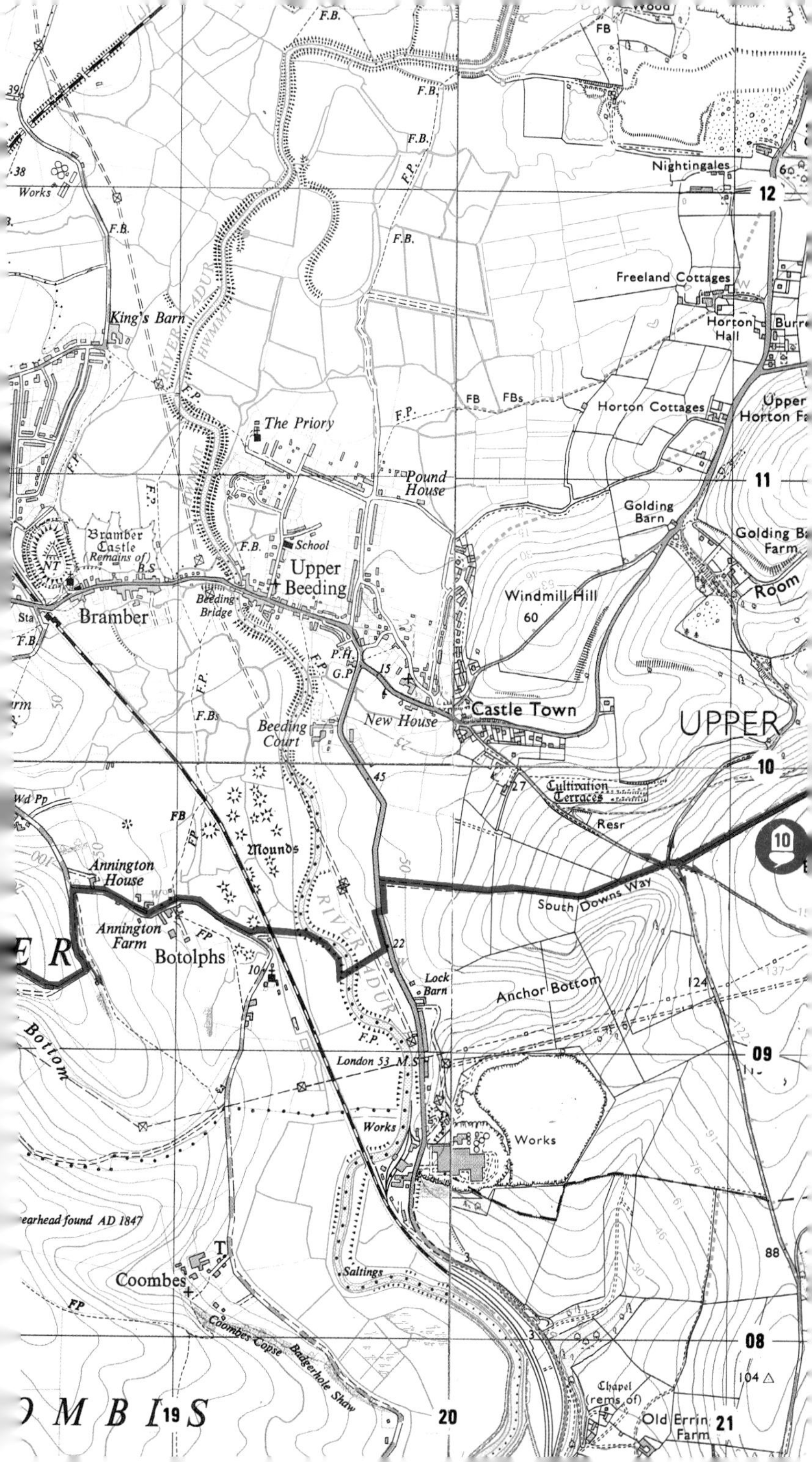

F.B.
Wood
FB
F.B.
F.B.
F.P.
Nightingales
12
39
38
Works
F.B.
F.B.
RIVER ADUR
HWMMT
Freeland Cottages
King's Barn
Horton Hall
F.P.
FB
FBs
Horton Cottages
Upper Horton Fa
The Priory
F.P.
Pound House
11
Golding Barn
Golding Ba Farm
Bramber Castle (Remains of)
NT
F.B.
School
B.S
Upper Beeding
Windmill Hill
60
Room
Beeding Bridge
Bramber
Sta
F.B.
P.H.
G.P.
15
F.P.
F.P.
Castle Town
UPPER
F.Bs
Beeding Court
New House
10
45
Wd Pp
27
Cultivation Terraces
Resr
FB
FP
Mounds
10
Annington House
South Downs Way
Annington Farm
FP
RIVER ADUR
Botolphs
22
E R
Lock Barn
Anchor Bottom
124
Bottom
F.P.
09
London 53 M.S
Works
Works
earhead found AD 1847
88
Coombes
Saltings
FP
Coombes Copse
Badgerhole Shaw
08
104
Chapel (rems of)
OMBIS
19
20
Old Errin Farm
21

Washington to Amberley

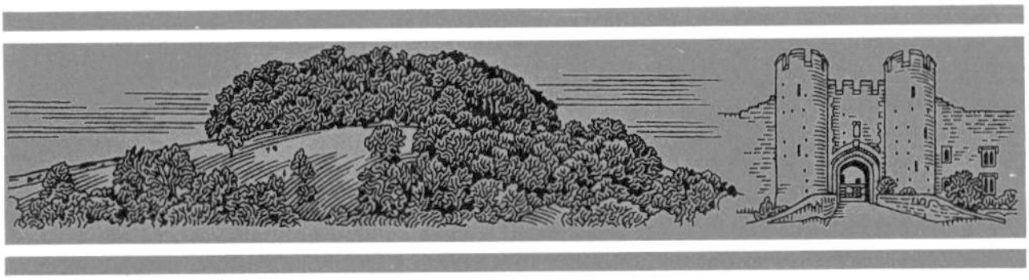

Distance 10½ kilometres

Rough parking among trees at the end of the previous section.

This section begins with alternative routes: 1. the direct route and 2. the detour through Washington. Each of the alternatives is a bridleway, but riders may prefer to follow the detour because it avoids the necessity of taking a horse across the busy dual carriageway of the A24 — there is a bridge at Washington. Riders are recommended to dismount and lead their horses across this bridge.

1. The direct route

From the end of the previous section, we cross the dual carriageway into Glaseby Lane, opposite, where there is a South Downs Way sign. This narrow, surfaced lane climbs steeply, bordered by tall bushes, with a few houses beside it. Near the top of the hill the surface gives way to rough gravel, with a fence on the right and an open arable field on the left. Beyond the fence are the ash trees of Biggen Holt, while to the south, beyond the field, are the woods of Highden Beeches. The track continues, wide and evident, with views of Chanctonbury Ring to the east and of the track ascending it.

The map shows three dykes crossing the track, but there is little of them to be seen on the ground. The track goes on over the summit of Barnsfarm Hill and in 3 kilometres from the A24, among cornfields, we find the junction with the detour from Washington. There is a South Downs Way signpost pointing the way forward and back; it marks the detour simply as 'bridleway'.

2. The detour through Washington

Opposite Glaseby Lane, instead of crossing the dual carriageway, you may turn north along the older road that at first runs parallel with the A24. It leads into the village of Washington, on a hillside. Turn left into the street called 'The Street', and proceed up to Washington church. Pass to the left of this, not neglecting to look in to see the little Byne monument dated 1600 on the interior wall of the tower, and note outside the tracery filling the sound-windows in the fifteenth-century tower.

Beyond the church the Way crosses a modern bridge over the A24 and continues to a junction, where we turn right, following the sign to Rowdell House. Rowdell is an old house of stone, re-windowed and re-roofed. In front of it we turn left into a short green lane beneath trees, which we leave between posts or through a gate. Do not ride a horse between the posts — there is a projecting screw that will score

Fruiting twigs of trees and shrubs of the chalk lands:
1 Spindle Tree; 2 Juniper;
3 Whitebeam; 4 Purging Buckthorn

Lane to Rowdell House, below the downs at Washington

its flanks. We cross into a surfaced lane and follow it uphill. It bends right into a wood, at the top of which is a gate. Beyond this we follow a hedged grassy track to a field gate. The way now is clear, through arable fields, joining a fence for a time, before running unfenced to the junction with route 1.

Following the combined ways west, we come to another bridleway turning off north, with a gate and a cattle-grid; its track can be seen swerving along the side of Sullington Hill as it descends towards Sullington. The nose of Sullington Hill was defended by a dyke.

A few steps beyond the cattle-grid a large black Dutch barn stands in a wired enclosure. We pass beside it to another cattle-grid and gate and a South Downs Way signpost. Wide panoramas of the Weald are seen from the track; they include rosy-coloured sandpits, which provide a contrast with the white of the downland chalk quarries.

The track climbs gently to the Chantry Post, which points to Lee Farm, Washington, Storrington, and Amberley. Chantry Post is a notable viewpoint for the Weald, the Forest Ridge, and the distant North Downs, and there are benches from which you may enjoy the view in comfort. A road comes up from Storrington and there is parking for several cars.

Storrington is a small town 4 kilometres north of the Way with a restored church in which is a brass of Henry Wilsha, a priest who died in 1591.

The way continues from Chantry Post with a fence on the left. Shortly the fence veers off to the south and we continue forward on the plain gravelled track, over the flank of Kithurst Hill; on the summit of the hill, at 213 metres, there is a triangulation point. There is a well known Celtic field system on the southern flank of the hill.

We go forward and find another road coming up from the north, from the B2139 near Springhead Farm; there is parking for many cars where it meets the Way. A bridleway goes south over Wepham Down to Burpham, from which the Youth Hostel at Warningcamp may be reached, 4½ kilometres from the Way.

Burpham is a village of interest, with an earthwork that may be the site of a Saxon burgh. It stands by the Arun, with views of Arundel castle to the west. The church is of various periods, but has some fine Norman work and some fourteenth-century benches. A prehistoric boat found near here in 1852 is in the keep of Lewes castle.

From the car park on the Way we climb gently on a broad track up to the summit of Springhead Hill and through a small wood, mostly of beeches. Beyond the wood the plainer track goes forward to Burpham, while we bear right to pass between wooden posts beside an iron gate. In the field to the north is a distinct barrow, still standing a couple of metres high, with a clump of wind-blown oaks beside it.

The track is wire-fenced on both sides. It crosses Rackham Hill with little sense of climbing, though the triangulation point on the left is 193 metres above sea level. There are fine views over the Weald and over the curious level marshland known as Amberley Wild Brooks — 'Wild' here means 'Weald' — which is divided into fields not by hedges but by dykes. East of Amberley Wild Brooks stretches the tree-populated Parham Park, which contains the large Elizabethan house of Parham. The house, which contains a fine collection of portraits, furniture, and needlework, is open to the public. Parham church, south of the house, dates from the fourteenth century and contains another lead font, the most recent of the three in Sussex; it is dated 1351. As we descend we pass through Rackham Banks, the only one of the many cross dykes marked on the map along the Way that is obvious as a bank and ditch; it still looks formidable. A bridleway through a gate follows the bottom of the ditch down towards the B2139. South of the Way it goes to Wepham Down.

The Way runs on between fences on a gentle descent towards Amberley Mount, passing the sites of tumuli in the corn. Except for the view we scarcely notice Amberley Mount; it looks more distinctive from the valley. After passing a stile and a gate we descend more rapidly beside a fence on the right, and come on to a rolled chalk track, which soon bears off left to Downs Farm. We go straight ahead through a stile with a gate and follow a narrowing track to a bridle-gate. Beyond this gate we descend to a road, down a short, steep chalk slide that needs care with horses, particularly as it comes out directly on to a road leading to the Amberley to Houghton road.

We turn left on this road, and soon have a view of Amberley village, with its church and twin-towered castle gatehouse. Amberley is a village of great charm. The manor of Amberley is said to have belonged to the see of Chichester before the Conquest, and the bishops built the castle as a summer residence. The walls enclose a picturesque sixteenth-century house and some modern buildings. The nearby church is good Norman, with some fine later work, including a fourteenth-century south doorway. There are some wall-paintings, an hour-glass stand by the pulpit, and a brass of 1424 with a rare enamelled tabard.

Farther on the South Downs Way road runs between two chalk-pits, now an industrial archaeology museum, well screened by hedges and marked by 'Danger' signs. Gaps in the hedges allow one to see that the road in fact runs on a knife-edge with high cliffs dropping on each side to the far depths of the chalk-pits. A left turn at a junction brings us on to the main road.

The road leads to Amberley station, on the London-Portsmouth line. Bus services are infrequent — a prior study of the timetable is advised. You may have to return to Storrington for a bus.

Dog fox

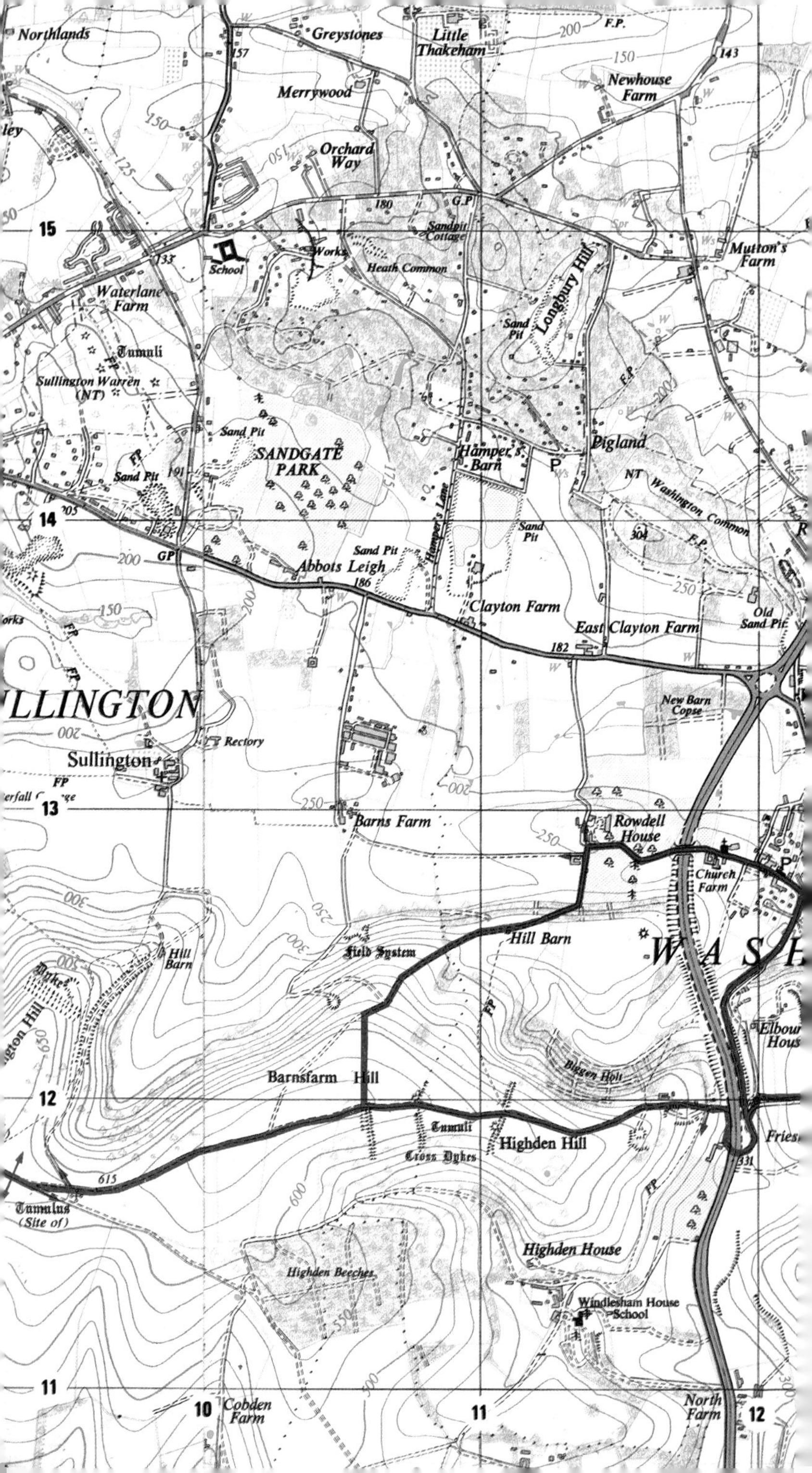
Northlands
Greystones
Little Thakeham
F.P.
200
157
150
143
Newhouse Farm
Merrywood
ley
150
Orchard Way
125
150
180
G.P
Sandpit Cottage
15
Works
Spr
Mutton's Farm
School
133
Heath Common
Longbury Hill
Waterlane Farm
Sand Pit
Tumuli
Sullington Warren (NT)
F.P.
200
Sand Pit
SANDGATE PARK
Pigland
Hamper's Barn
P
FP
Sand Pit
191
NT
Washington Common
175
205
14
Sand Pit
304
Hamper's Lane
GP
200
Sand Pit
Abbots Leigh
186
F.P.
250
200
150
Clayton Farm
Old Sand Pit
Works
East Clayton Farm
FP
182
FP
LLINGTON
New Barn Copse
200
Rectory
Sullington
FP
250
200
13
Barns Farm
Rowdell House
250
Church Farm
P
300
250
300
Hill Barn
Hill Barn
Field System
W A S H
Dyke
FP
650
Elbou Hous
Biggen Holt
Barnsfarm Hill
12
Tumuli
Highden Hill
Fries
331
Cross Dykes
615
FP
Tumulus (Site of)
600
Highden House
Highden Beeches
550
Windlesham House School
300
11
10
Cobden Farm
11
North Farm
12
300

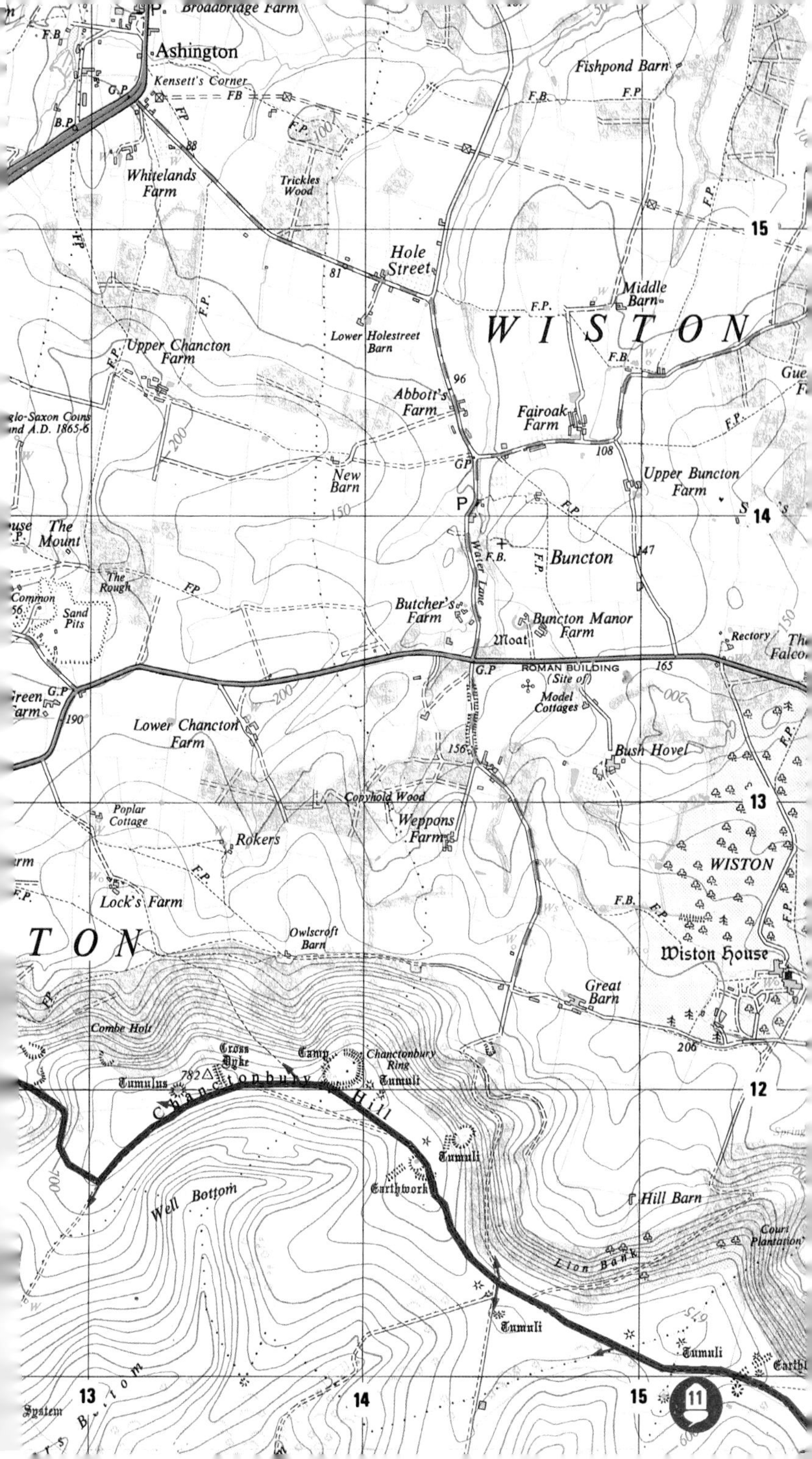

Broadbridge Farm
Ashington
F.B
Kensett's Corner
FB
G.P
B.P
FP
88
Whitelands Farm
F.P.
100
Trickles Wood
Fishpond Barn
F.B.
F.P
15
Hole Street
81
Middle Barn
F.P.
WISTON
Lower Holestreet Barn
F.B.
Upper Chancton Farm
96
Abbott's Farm
Fairoak Farm
Anglo-Saxon Coins
and A.D. 1865-6
200
108
GP
New Barn
Upper Buncton Farm
P
150
14
The Mount
F.B.
Water Lane
Buncton
147
The Rough
FP
Common
Sand Pits
Butcher's Farm
Buncton Manor Farm
Moat
Rectory
G.P
ROMAN BUILDING
(Site of)
165
Model Cottages
Green Farm
G.P.
190
200
Lower Chancton Farm
156
Bush Hovel
13
Poplar Cottage
Copyhold Wood
Weppons Farm
Rokers
WISTON
F.P.
Lock's Farm
F.B.
Owlscroft Barn
TON
Wiston House
Great Barn
206
Combe Holt
Cross Dyke
Camp
Chanctonbury Ring
782
Tumulus
Chanctonbury Hill
Tumuli
12
Tumuli
Earthwork
Well Bottom
Hill Barn
Court Plantation
Lion Bank
700
Tumuli
675
Tumuli
13
14
15
System
11
600

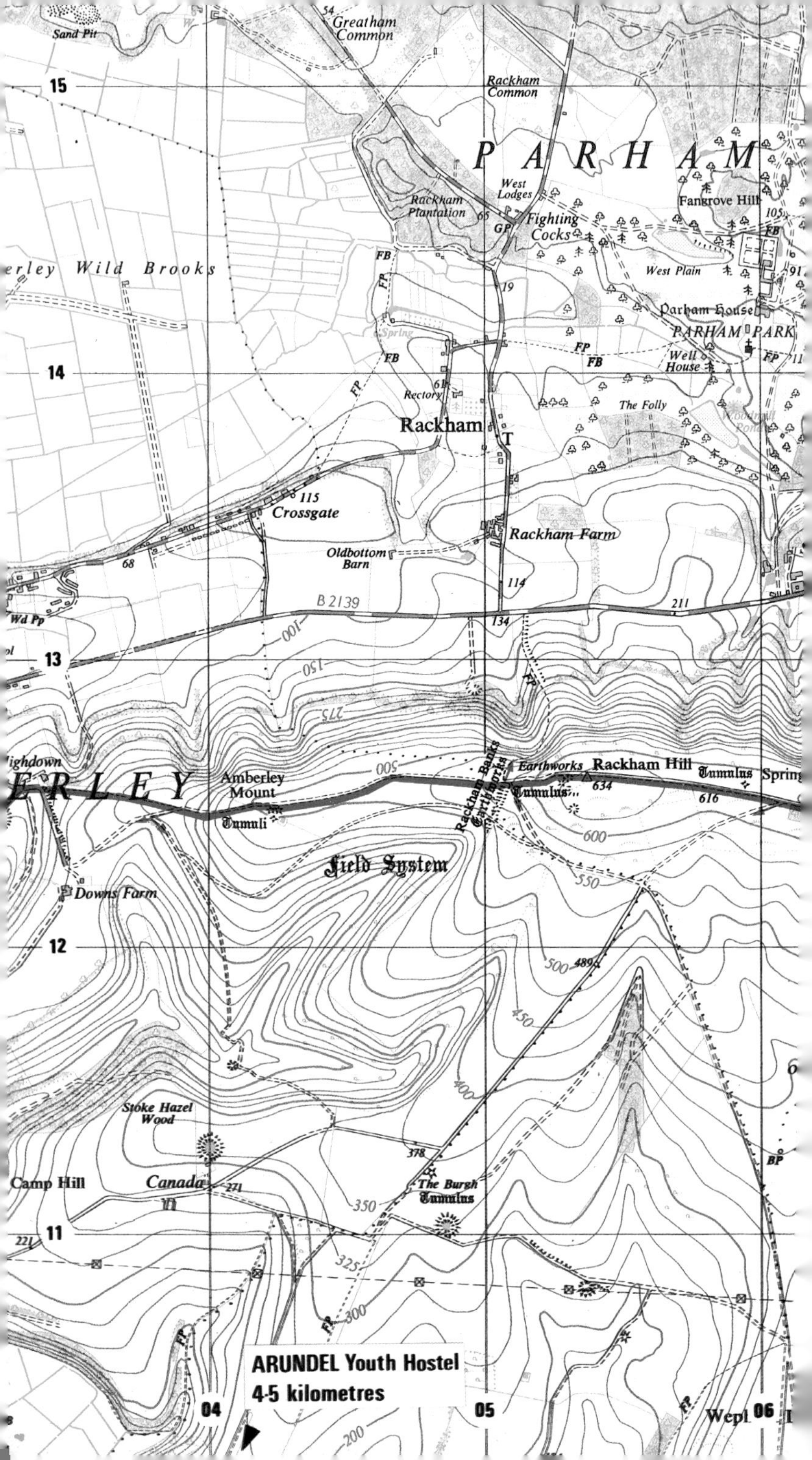

Sand Pit
Greatham Common
Rackham Common
P A R H A M
West Lodges
Rackham Plantation
Fighting Cocks
Fangrove Hill
West Plain
erley Wild Brooks
Parham House
PARHAM PARK
Well House
Rectory
Rackham
The Folly
Crossgate
Rackham Farm
Oldbottom Barn
B 2139
Wd Pp
Amberley Mount
Tumuli
Earthworks
Rackham Hill
Tumulus
Rackham Banks
Earthworks
Spring
ERLEY
Field System
Downs Farm
Stoke Hazel Wood
Camp Hill
Canada
The Burgh
Tumulus
BP
15
14
13
12
11
04
05
06
ARUNDEL Youth Hostel
4·5 kilometres

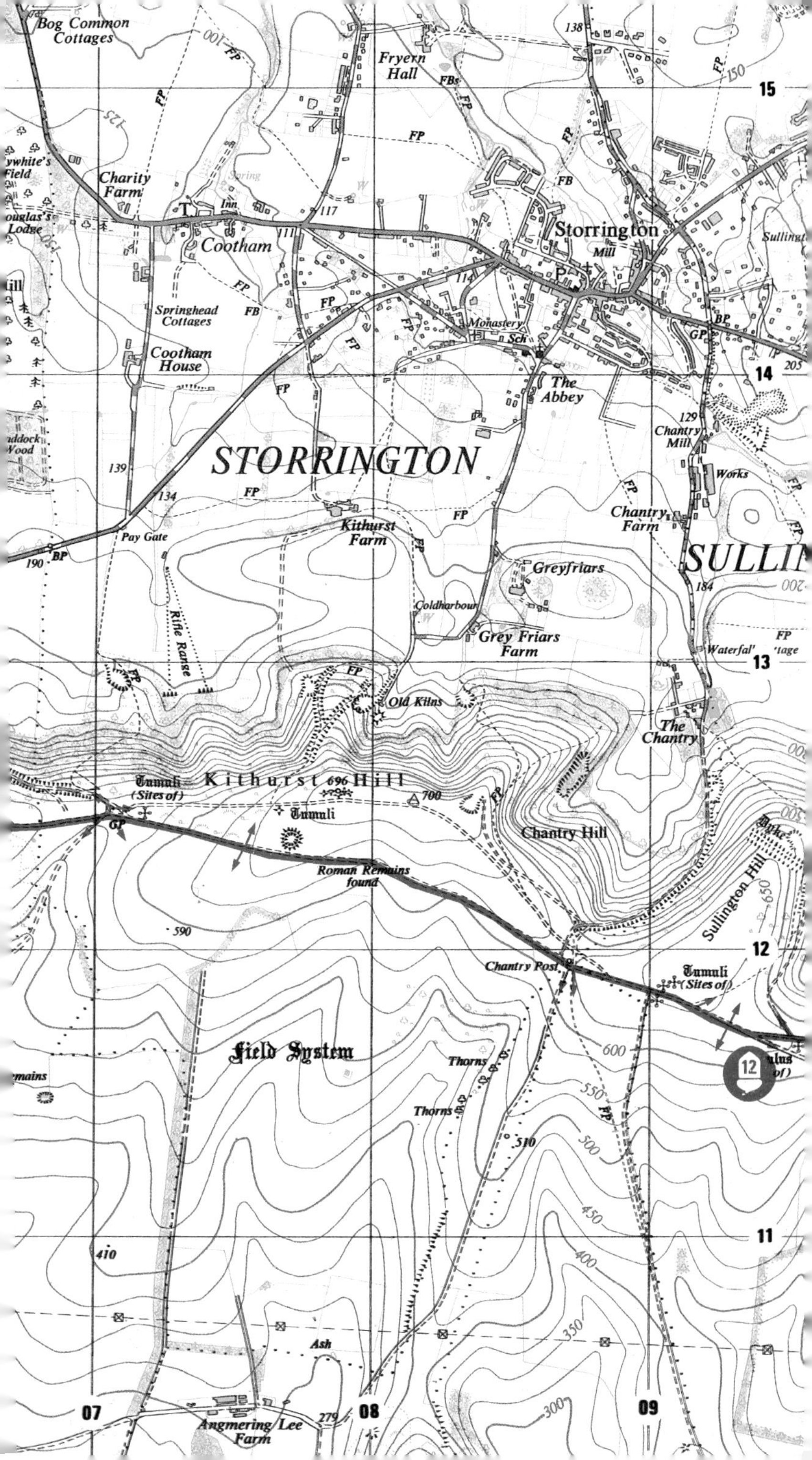
Bog Common Cottages
Fryern Hall
FBs
FP
Charity Farm
Spring
Inn
Cootham
Douglas's Lodge
Storrington
Mill
Springhead Cottages
FB
Monastery
Sch
Cootham House
The Abbey
Chantry Mill
Works
STORRINGTON
Kithurst Farm
Chantry Farm
SULLI
Pay Gate
BP
GP
Greyfriars
Coldharbour
Grey Friars Farm
Rifle Range
Waterfall
Old Kilns
The Chantry
Tumuli (Sites of)
Kithurst 696 Hill
700
Tumuli
Chantry Hill
Dyke
Roman Remains found
Sullington Hill
Chantry Post
Field System
Thorns
Ash
Angmering Lee Farm
Remains
07
08
09
11
12
13
14
15

Amberley to Cocking

Distance $17\frac{3}{4}$ kilometres

Parking in the station car park.

Coming from Amberley station yard turn left into the road to Houghton. Here is a side road to North Stoke, an isolated village in the southward extension of the Wild Brooks, in a loop of the Arun; it has an interesting thirteenth- and fourteenth-century cruciform church. South Stoke, its twin village, is only $\frac{3}{4}$ kilometre away by footpath, over a bridge across the Arun, but by road the villages are many miles apart. South Stoke has a church basically Norman. Both villages are very ancient, for 'stoke' is from the Saxon.

Shortly after leaving Amberley station the road passes over Houghton bridge across the Arun. Motor-cruisers use this limpid stretch of the river, and level fields extend to the foot of the hills. Houghton village is set beyond the levels, where the road rises, on a site safe above floods. The little flint church beside the road is plain Early English in style, built in the thirteenth century; it has a brass of 1496 and the churchyard is full of eighteenth-century headstones. Charles II is reputed to have stopped for refreshment at the timber-framed George and Dragon Inn, during his flight to the Continent in October 1651.

After passing the church we turn right at the top of the hill into the road to Bury and Bignor. Facing us here is a restored timber-framed and thatched cottage. We go down past its gable and in less than $\frac{3}{4}$ kilometre turn left by a South Downs Way signpost into a field. We are on a wide chalky track between arable fields. We follow the fence on the right uphill, and bear right, with, behind us, an improving view of the Arun meandering through its valley, and the hills of Amberley beyond, in which is a hillside eaten away by vast quarries.

Where the fence ends the track bears left up the hill, touching a corner of Coombe Wood.

In $\frac{3}{4}$ kilometre we pass space for rough parking beneath trees and come out on to the busy A29. Crossing this road we go north for a few metres to a signed chalk track on the left. There are, in fact, various tracks starting here, but they fuse together within a short distance. The surface of all of them is rough and stony. The fused path continues as a broad and chalky rutted track. It comes to a junction, with the track to the left going towards a deep, dark wood of mixed trees — oak, sycamore, etc., with a lot of travellers' joy and ivy; this is Houghton Forest and we must avoid going into it — so we take the right-hand track at the junction. This runs a field distant from the edge of the forest.

As the forest recedes on the left two radio masts come in sight on a distant hill. We pass through the two gates and the way becomes grassed over and rutted. It improves a little as it descends Westburton Hill towards two barns of corrugated iron. Passing these barns, the path forward seems to be one that climbs the opposite hillside beside a high hawthorn hedge, but, obeying the South Downs Way signs, we make a sudden zigzag left and right and climb the hillside on the other side of this hedge. The fences and hedges here are festooned with bindweed, the delicate pink trumpets rayed with white. The path now climbs very steeply for about ¾ kilometre, to a junction with a wider track. Here we turn right and climb more gently towards what seem to be several gateposts on the horizon. They turn out to be posts arranged round the Toby's Stone. This is a monument in the form of a large mounting-block, whose presence here is explained in its inscription: '1888–1955 James Wentworth Fitzwilliam-Toby, Secretary Cowdray Hounds 1922–1930, British Field Sports Society 1930–1953, Master of Foxhounds Association 1945–1955. Here he lies where he longed to be.' The other side of the block commemorates his wife Beryl, who died in 1960. Perhaps Toby's spirit still enjoys the beautiful view over the trees of the scarp to the woods and fields of the Weald and the villages of Bignor, Sutton, and Barlavington, and many others. Behind the block is an iron sign, a thick chunk of metal like a small tombstone, with the letters FL on it; it is probably an estate boundary marker of Squire Fletcher of Dale Park.

Farther on, the Way passes the summit of Bignor Hill, 225 metres. Bignor Hill belongs to the National Trust as part of the 1,400 hectare Slindon estate bequeathed by Mr J. F. Wootton Isaacson in 1950. It includes the neolithic causewayed camp of Barkhale south of the Way.

Pheasants are seen frequently on this part of the Way, with occasional partridges.

We come from Bignor Hill over a cattle-grid with a gate beside it. The South Downs Way crosses the Roman Stane Street here and a surfaced road comes up from Bignor. In fine weather there are usually a number of people here as there is parking for several cars. Stane Street, built in the early years of the Roman conquest to connect London and Chichester, was one of the important highways of the south east. Its course from Chichester to the South Downs Way is easily traced on the map as a straight line — part of it is the modern A285. Near the parking area a large signpost once stood on a round barrow, its arms pointing to Slindon, Regnum (Chichester), Sutton, Bignor, and Londinium.

At Bignor, 3 kilometres north west, there was a Roman villa of some importance, with interesting mosaic floors, which were rediscovered in 1811 and are now on show. Bignor church was Norman, but it was rebuilt in the thirteenth century, retaining the Norman chancel arch.

The South Downs Way is signed along a stony white track, passing among various kinds of bushes towards two large radio masts. Before the masts are reached the Way is signed to the left, along the north western side of the agger, or raised bank, which marks the line of Stane Street. We walk with Roman history for a hundred metres or so as we follow the agger towards the south west. Then the Way is signed to the right to follow a headland fence.

After passing a stone cattle-trough on the right we take the right-hand one of the two wide openings and go ahead with a fence on the left hand. There are extensive views to the south, with the sea in sight. We pass into a field with a large wood on the right and cross over two not very obvious dykes. The Way deteriorates to a double stony track along the edge of the wood, with quantities of travellers' joy on the bushes, and tall clumps of marjoram.

At the end of the field we come to a cattle-grid and a gate, and afterwards another grid and gate. You may come upon scores of pheasants in this area. As it descends the track becomes smooth chalk, and does a zigzag to follow pylons for a few metres before resuming its original direction down towards Littleton Farm. As we descend, a track is visible on the face of the opposite down — a mere thin line wandering up the hill. It may not look like it, but this is our route. We reach it by turning right on the A285 Duncton road opposite the farm and then turning left into a tree-shaded lane, marked by a South Downs Way signpost. We follow this lane, ignoring the concrete track going off to the left, and come to a gate leading on to a wide crossing footpath. A few metres beyond is another similar gate into an arable field. The path through this field and the next field may be found not to have been reinstated after ploughing, in which case you will have to tread it out, keeping as straight up the hill as you can, and bearing slightly right. The first field has a bridle-gate at the upper end, while the second is terminated by a wood, to which you come bearing a little left. Notice, incidentally, how very stony these two fields are.

The climb through the fields is onerous, and no wonder, for we are coming up to Littleton Down with Crown Tegleaze, at 255 metres the highest point of the Sussex Downs, near-by.

The wood at the top of the field has a carpet of St John's wort and the trees are mostly beeches.

A few metres on we come to the Tegleaze signpost in a clearing among bushes and trees. It points south-west to East Dean and north-east to Duncton and in the two directions of the South Downs Way.

Now begins a long length of the South Downs Way that is of more interest to the botanist, and perhaps the entomologist, than it is to the general walker or rider. From here for many miles the Way passes through woodland or is confined between bushes so that views are rare and it is not evident that the track runs on high land. The ground beneath our feet changes from chalk to clay and loam in the woods. We are so far from popular haunts that crops of blackberries, very profuse in a good season, remain unpicked, and sloes and bullaces ripen unregarded.

Over Graffham Down woods have been cut down in places in preparation for fields, but yew trees have been left untouched, and so too have the bordering bushes of the track. Rabbits are common enough, and with luck you may come upon deer — woodlands are the home of the dappled fallow deer.

In one place the designer of the Way has taken the opportunity for gentle humour. A finger-post suddenly points to the right, out of the lane. Within a few metres we are directed left along a track that shortly comes back into the original lane again. This kink or zigzag gives a brief respite from claustrophobia. There is a path from here down to Graffham church, 3 kilometres north.

On our left a notice-board beside a gate announces the Forestry Commission's Charlton Forest. A public bridleway goes from the gate down a broad ride between the trees.

For a brief moment the Way has a sudden view of distant hills to the north. Shortly afterwards the track takes a left-hand turn and turns again through a gate on the right. It comes out of the enclosing trees, but Charlton Forest, dark and sombre among the closely planted beeches, still continues on the left, beyond a fence masked by bindweed. There are bridleways and footpaths through the forest, going south towards Singleton, some 4 kilometres distant, a charming flint-built village with a church mostly Perpendicular, but retaining a Saxon tower. Next to the village is the hillside site of the Weald and Downland Open-Air Museum, recognised by the Countryside Commission as a country park, in which cottages, mills, farmhouses, etc., have been brought from their original sites and re-erected; it is well worth a visit.

A triangulation point on the right marks the summit of Heyshott Down at 234 metres. Heyshott is a small village with an Early English church. The name 'Heyshott' means the *sceat* or strip of land where heather grows, and this is interesting because in this district heather will be seen growing beside the path — the only place in the long trajectory of the South Downs Way where the clayey soil is sufficiently acid to support it.

We come to a crossing bridleway, which comes over a field from the north and to the south goes into the wood. We go straight ahead through a field gate and come clear of trees at last and fully into the open. As we descend the flank of Manorfarm Down and enter Hillbarn Lane the continuation of the South Downs Way ahead is visible up the slope of the down on the far side of the valley in which the A286 runs from Cocking to Singleton. It may be seen that for the first part the Way is a lane between hedges.

Cocking, 1½ kilometres north, is a charming little village with a Norman church at the foot of the steep climb up Cocking Hill. If you are leaving the Way to visit Cocking, a bridleway from Hill Barn Farm avoids the tarmac.

There is a bus stop where Hillbarn Lane joins the road. Buses to Midhurst, Singleton, and Chichester.

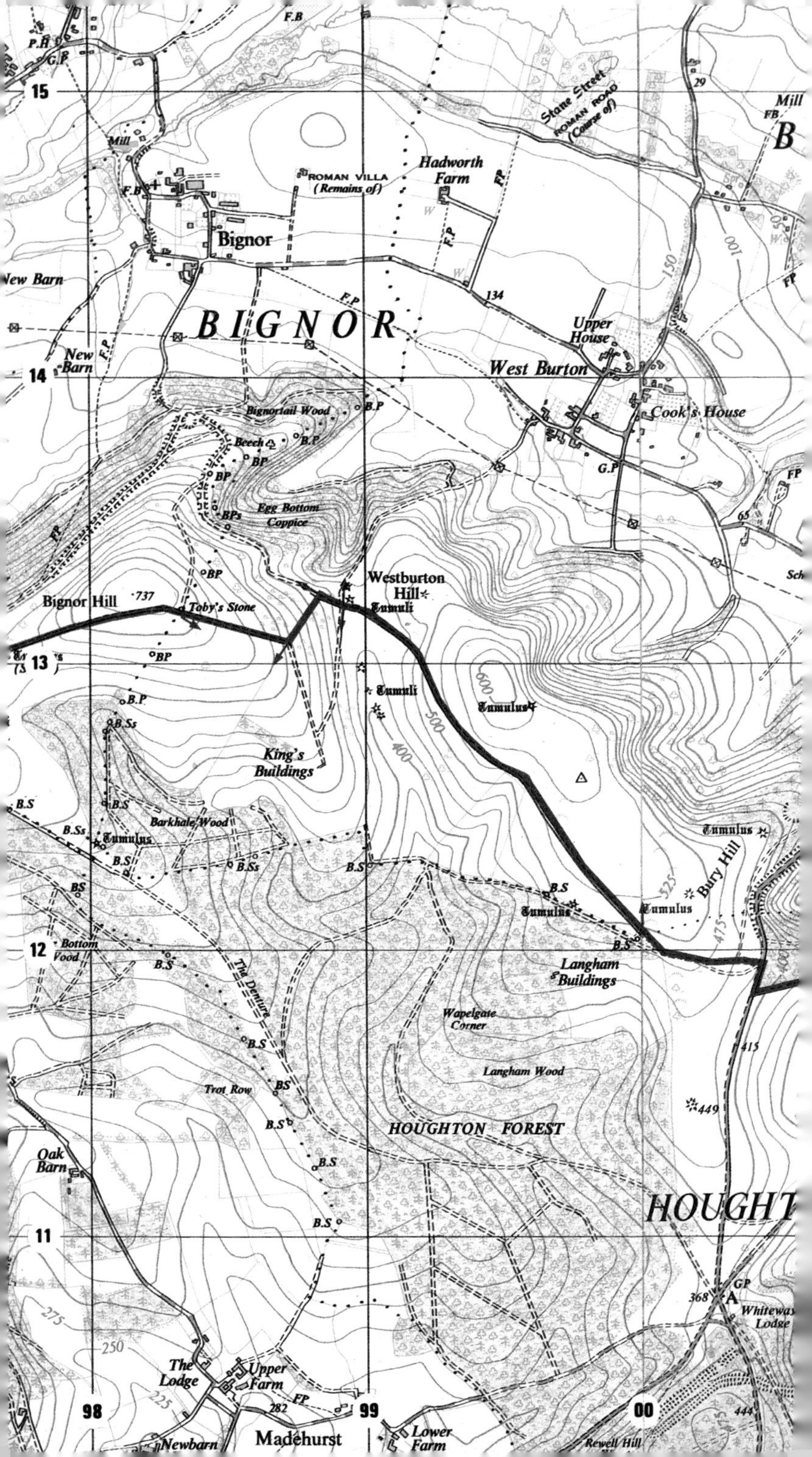

Bignor
BIGNOR
ROMAN VILLA (Remains of)
Hadworth Farm
Stane Street
ROMAN ROAD (Course of)
New Barn
Mill
Upper House
West Burton
Cook's House
Bignortail Wood
Beech
Egg Bottom Coppice
Westburton Hill
Tumuli
Bignor Hill
737
Toby's Stone
Tumulus
King's Buildings
Barkhale Wood
Bury Hill
Bottom Wood
The Denture
Langham Buildings
Wapelgate Corner
Langham Wood
Trot Row
HOUGHTON FOREST
Oak Barn
HOUGHT
Whiteway Lodge
The Lodge
Upper Farm
Madehurst
Newbarn
Lower Farm
Rewell Hill
15
14
13
12
11
98
99
00

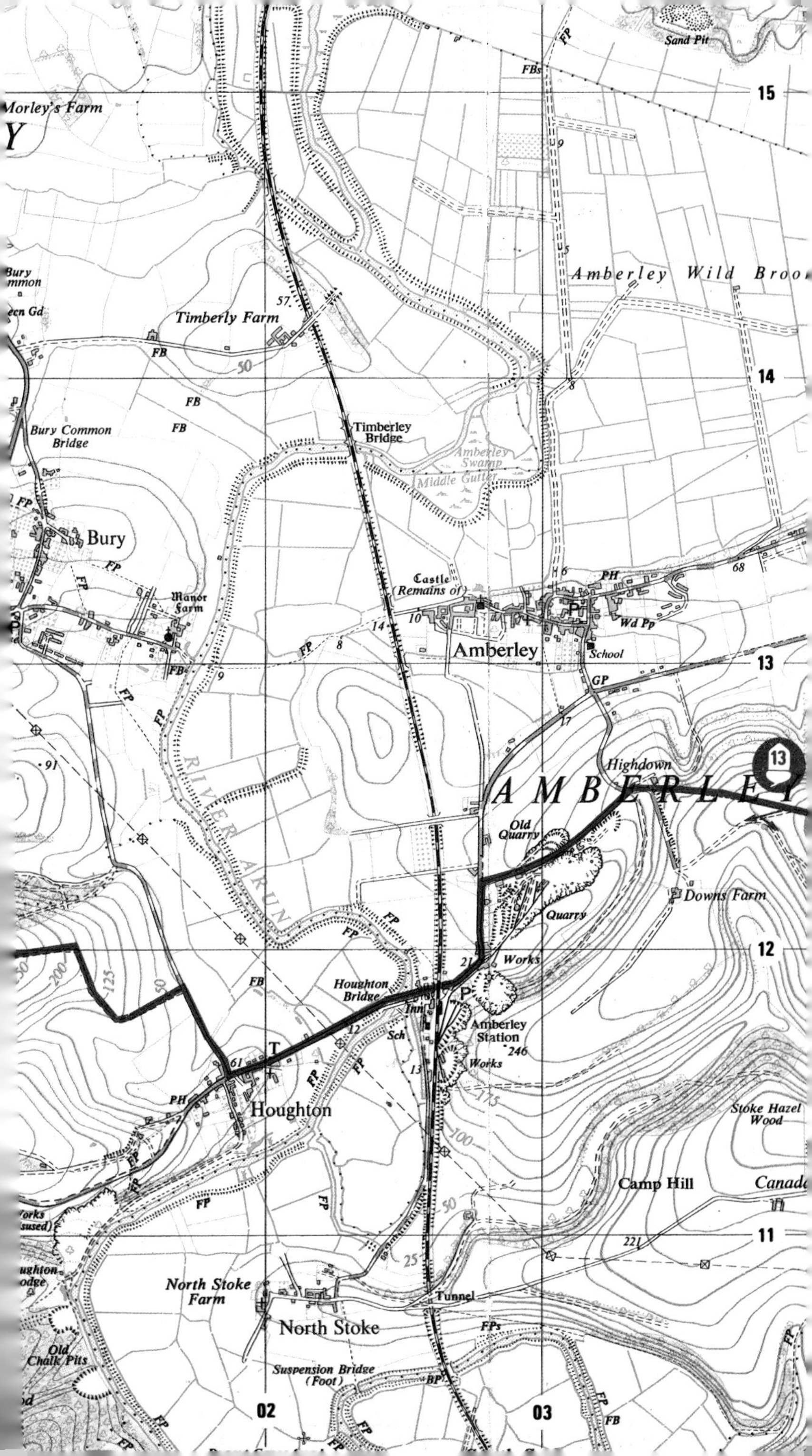

Sand Pit
FP
FBs
15
Morley's Farm
Bury Common
Timberly Farm
57
FB
50
14
Amberley Wild Broo
Bury Common Bridge
FB
Timberley Bridge
Amberley Swamp
Middle Gutter
Bury
FP
Castle (Remains of)
PH
68
Manor Farm
10
14
8
Amberley
Wd Pp
School
13
FP
9
GP
17
91
RIVER ARUN
Highdown
13
AMBERLEY
Old Quarry
Downs Farm
Quarry
Works
12
200
125
50
FB
Houghton Bridge
Inn
Amberley Station
246
Sch
Works
61
T
Houghton
PH
175
Stoke Hazel Wood
100
Camp Hill
Canada
FP
FP
50
11
221
25
North Stoke Farm
Tunnel
North Stoke
FPs
Old Chalk Pits
Suspension Bridge (Foot)
BP
02
03
FP
FB

F.P
The Gables
Calloways
Parson's Copse
17
EAST
LAVINGTO
School
Rectory
Lavington Stud Farm
Lodge
Oak
LAVINGTO
Seaford College
East Lavington
Lavin Hou
Limekiln Bottom
RAFFHAM DOWN
Tumulus
Beech
718
Dyke
16
WOOLAVINGTON
Dyke
Tegleaze Farm
Grass Tegleaze
Barn Tegleaze
Tumuli
FOREST
TEGLEAZE
Lamb Lea
Stickingspit Bottom
Crown Tegleaze
15
Littleton Down
Limekiln Bottom
760
Warren Bottom
North Side
800
700
Heath Hanger
North Down
668
Waltham Down
Tumuli
600
738
500
400
MALECOMB
14
Heath Hill
722
Church Farm
Upwaltham
354
Oxen Down
Lambdown Bottom
DEAN
UPWALTHAM
Droke Cottage
340
13
Combe Bottom
Droke
307
Bonney's Hangar
Upwaltham H
Droke Hanger
Tumulus
Astead Down
Stubbs Wood
Benges Wood
92
93
94

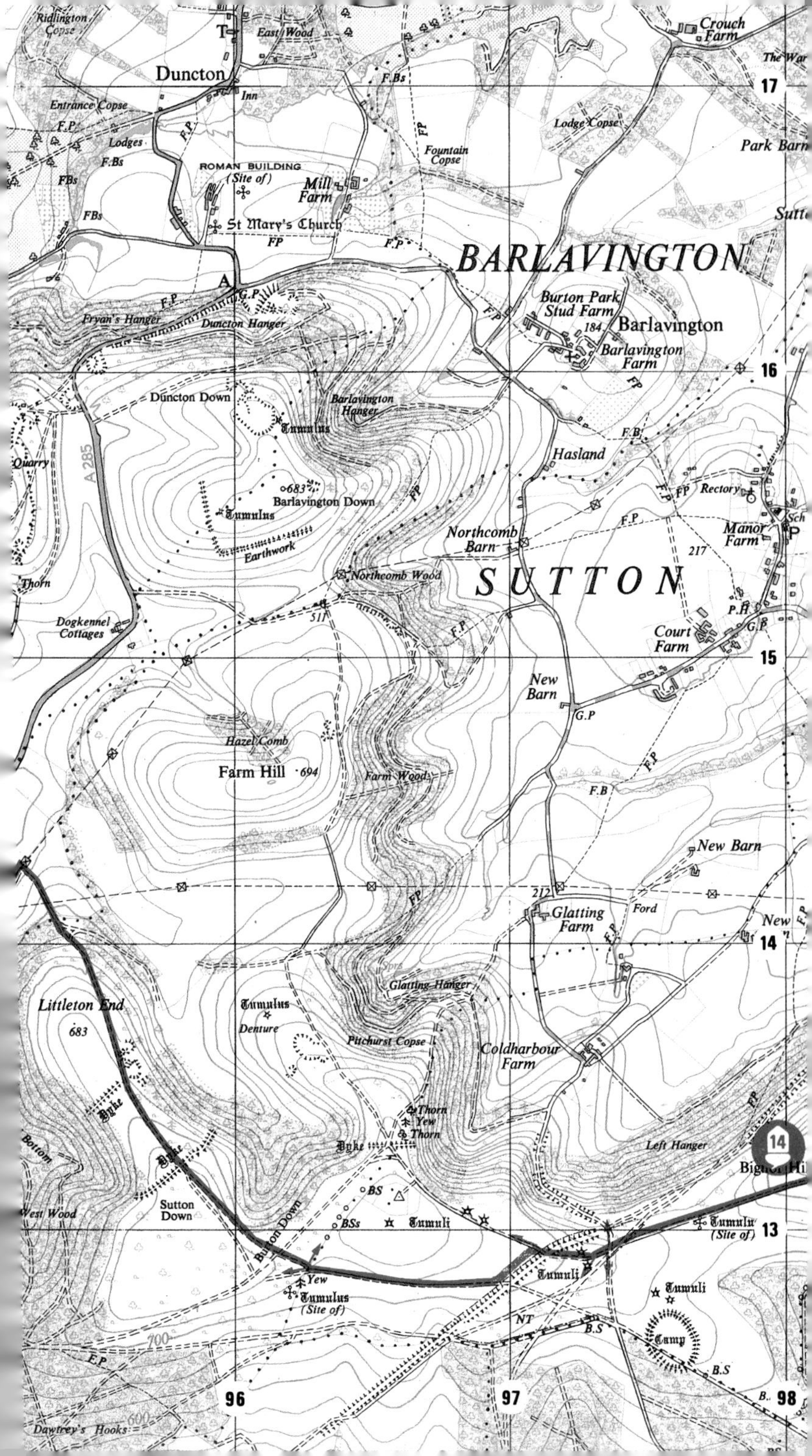

Ridlington Copse
Duncton
East Wood
Crouch Farm
The War
17
Inn
Entrance Copse
F.Bs
F.P
Lodges
Lodge Copse
Park Barn
Fountain Copse
ROMAN BUILDING
(Site of)
Mill Farm
St Mary's Church
FP
BARLAVINGTON
G.P
Burton Park Stud Farm
184
Barlavington
Barlavington Farm
Fryan's Hanger
Duncton Hanger
Duncton Down
16
Barlavington Hanger
Tumulus
F.B
Quarry
A 285
Hasland
683
Barlavington Down
Rectory
Tumulus
Northcomb Barn
Manor Farm
217
Earthwork
Northcomb Wood
SUTTON
Thorn
511
P.H
Dogkennel Cottages
Court Farm
15
New Barn
Hazel Comb
Farm Hill
694
Farm Wood
F.B
New Barn
212
Glatting Farm
Ford
14
Glatting Hanger
Littleton End
683
Tumulus
Denture
Pitchurst Copse
Coldharbour Farm
Dyke
Thorn
Yew
Thorn
Bottom
Dyke
Left Hanger
14
Sutton Down
BS
West Wood
BSs
Tumuli
13
Tumulus (Site of)
Bignor Hill
Burton Down
Yew
Tumuli
Tumulus (Site of)
Tumuli
NT
B.S
Camp
700
F.P
B.S
96
97
98
600
Dawtrey's Hooks

COCKING
18
Horley Farm
Bell Lane
Oldhouse Farm
Rectory
Sch
FP
Sage Barn
Cocking (P)
PH
New Barn
Sunwool Farm
Henley Lane
The Butts (Chalk Pit)
Crypt Farm
17
Quarry
FP
Cockinghill
Cocking Tunnel
Middlefield Lane
Hill Barn
Hillbarn Lane
Manorfarm Down
Tumulus (Site of)
Hoefield Lane
Highditch Copse
16
Herringdean Wood
Punters Copse
The Marlows
Wolverstone Farm
BS
A 286
Littlewood Plantation
Singleton Forest
435
Littlewood Farm
Nightingale Wood
15
Broadham Cottages
Burntoak Gate
Barn
Wellhanger Copse
Broadham Farm
Drove Tunnel
Drovers
Lady Wood
Hill Cottages
238
FP
14
Levin Down
558
Holly
512
Hat Hill
Cucumber Farm
North Lane
NT
SINGLETO
Chills Down
87
Rectory
88
89
Field System
Railway

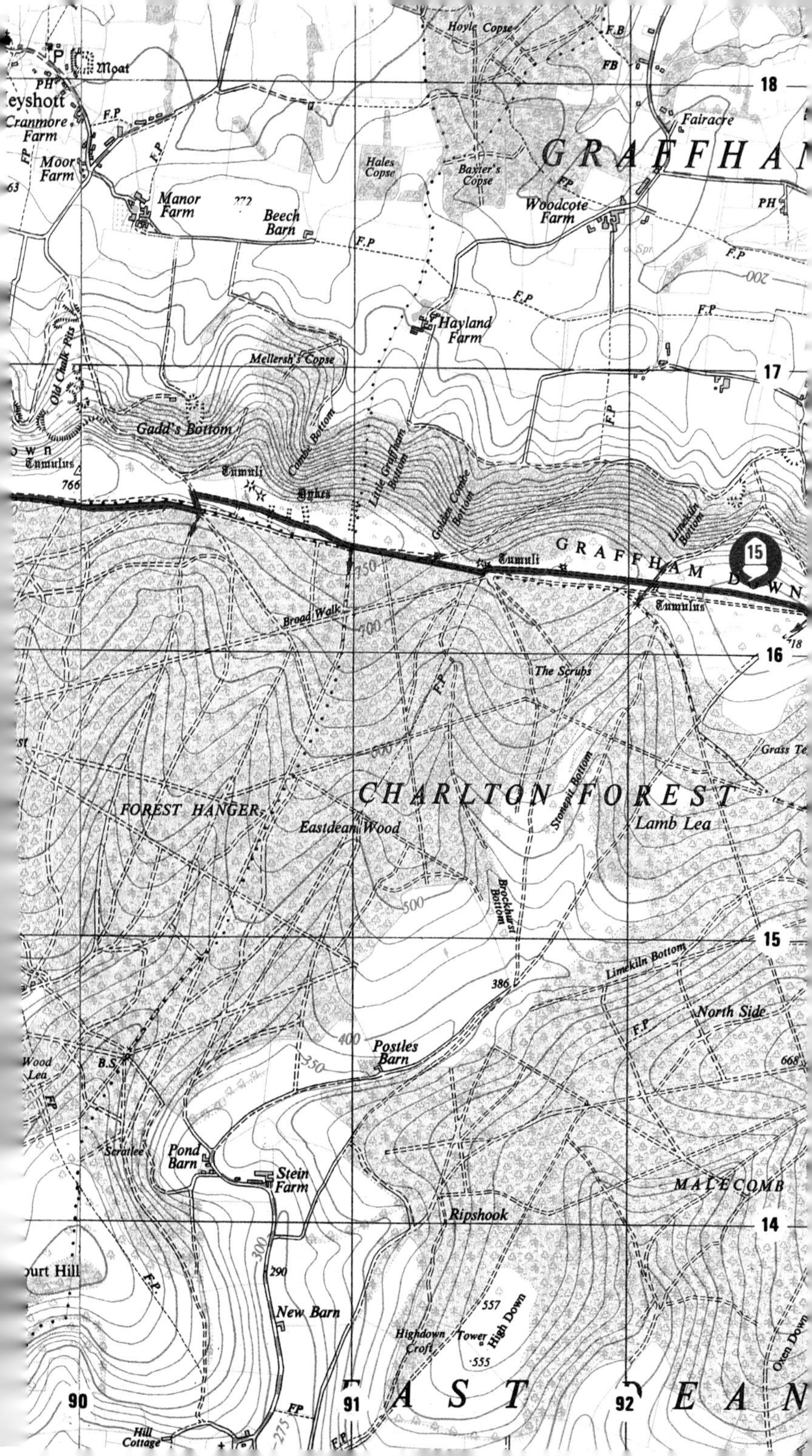

Hoyle Copse
F.B
FB
Moat
PH
eyshott
Cranmore Farm
F.P
Moor Farm
63
18
Fairacre
GRAFFHAM
Hales Copse
Baxter's Copse
Manor Farm
272
Beech Barn
Woodcote Farm
PH
Spr
200
Hayland Farm
Mellersh's Copse
Old Chalk Pits
17
Gadd's Bottom
Combe Bottom
Little Graffham Bottom
Golden Combe Bottom
Tumulus
Tumuli
766
Dykes
Limekiln Bottom
GRAFFHAM DOWN
15
750
Tumulus
Broad Walk
700
18
16
The Scrubs
Grass Te
CHARLTON FOREST
FOREST HANGER
Eastdean Wood
Stonepit Bottom
Lamb Lea
650
500
Brockhurst Bottom
386
Limekiln Bottom
North Side
400
Postles Barn
350
Wood Lea
B.S.
668
Scratlee
Pond Barn
Stein Farm
MALECOMB
Ripshook
14
ourt Hill
300
290
New Barn
557
High Down
Highdown Croft
Tower
555
Oxen Down
90
91
92
EAST DEAN
Hill Cottage
275

Cocking to Buriton

Distance $13\frac{1}{2}$ kilometres to county boundary; further $2\frac{1}{2}$ kilometres to Buriton

Unofficial parking for a couple of cars on the verge at the foot of Middlefield Lane.

Middlefield Lane begins opposite the foot of Hillbarn Lane, the end of the previous section. It passes between the flint and tile buildings of a farm and then begins to climb as a hedged lane bordered by elderberry, hawthorn, and dogwood. The surface becomes rougher as it ascends over Cocking Down. Creeping bellflower may be found in the hedge, with blue trumpets and long and narrow leaves. As the track comes to the top of Cocking Down the hedges become thinner and disappear. A crossing bridleway goes north east to Cocking by way of Crypt Farm, and south into the huge area of woodland that is to keep pace with us for miles, usually a field distant; it has several names, among which are Venus Wood, Bepton Wood, and Linchball Wood. There is no mistaking the South Downs Way. It is plain and evident as it pushes westwards and the excellent signposting is almost a work of supererogation.

There are expansive and breathtaking views of the Weald, and below the scarp the village of Cocking is seen, with its roofs lost and found among trees. We pass the woods of Stead Combe on our right and enter a lane between barbed-wire fences. In the field to the left are two barrows, and a few steps beyond we have a view to the south, over the conifers of Newfarm Plantation and Bepton Wood, of an extent of the south coast towards Selsey Bill, with the spire of Chichester cathedral making a vertical accent.

Ahead, along the Way, is Linch Down, with a triangulation point marking the second highest altitude of the Sussex Downs — 248 metres. Linch Down is all arable land and there appears to be no path to the trig. point from the Way. We miss what must be a superb viewpoint, but we are compensated in many places along this section of the track with some of the finest views over the Weald, in which, beyond the Midhurst country, the Bexley ridge appears, with Hindhead, Blackdown, and Leith Hill, and pale in the distance the North Downs.

West of Linch Down the marching conifers pour into a deep combe south of the track, and over their heads the view extends to Culver Cliff on the Isle of Wight.

A bridleway heads off north towards Bepton and the Way continues over Didling Hill, where another bridleway leaves for Didling. The Way enters a lane with thick scrub on one side and high wire-netting on the other. The wire fence encloses the grounds of

Looking east from Cocking Down

Monkton House, which is deeply hidden among its trees and bushes and is miles distant from a main road. The owners keep exotic fowl, hence the wire-netting.

The Way enters a wood on the slopes of Treyford Hill. It passes the southern end of a line of five Bronze Age bell barrows known as the Devil's Jumps; they are so well concealed in the scrub that you may not realise they are there.

Beyond the Devil's Jumps the trees of the wood are taller and are mostly beeches. Here, on Philliswood Down, we find a crossing of bridleways in the wood. The track ahead, leading southwards, goes down to Hooksway and North Marden, one of four Marden villages in this area. A four-armed South Downs Way sign points our way to the right. Shortly the track emerges from the wood and divides, but the two tracks converge later on. A bridleway coming out of the wood from Philliswood Farm and Hooksway converges from the left.

The Way descends as a wide track, chalky and stony, and then ascends to a T junction. Here we turn left towards Buriton Farm, but for only a few steps to a bridle-gate on the right. The Way now runs alongside an arable field with a fence on the left, beyond which are the flint and tile buildings of the farm. A farm gate leads into a narrow track just wide enough for a horse, and we come out at last on to more open down along the lower edge of an arable field. A woodland to the right is largely of ash trees, and beyond is the Weald. We go over a crossing bridleway, which goes north to Elsted, through a gate, and south to Hooksway once more.

Beyond the crossing, the Way turns sharply left and begins to climb steeply up Pen Hill, alongside a field that, despite its slope, is arable. On our right is a ditch or dyke and the track appears to run on an embankment that has all but worn away. This is the earth-work 1½ kilometres long shown on the map, extending over Pen Hill, down into a hollow, and up again towards the summit of Beacon Hill. It does not appear that it can have been defensive; it was probably an Iron Age or Saxon boundary line.

From the breathless summit of Pen Hill we see the massive shape of Beacon Hill ahead and close at hand, with the earthworks of the Iron Age fort apparent but not impressive. From the base of Pen Hill worn chalk tracks climb Beacon Hill and this is the way for the energetic amateur of views; but it is not the official route of the South Downs Way. The Beacon Hill route, which is a short cut, rejoins the way at a signpost on the other side of the hill. From Pen Hill the South Downs Way may be seen turning left at the foot of Beacon Hill to climb aslant the down, parallel with but below the rampart of the fort. It comes to a level near an unwelcome landmark, an old, rusty, four-wheeled iron caravan used as a shepherd's hut. In front of it a South Downs Way signpost confirms our direction forwards to a field gate into a lane. Half a dozen steps down this lane and we turn right beside a South Downs Way signpost into a narrow lane bordered by blackberry bushes, clumps of furze, and tall stands of rosebay willowherb.

The track descends aslant the rough, grassy, western side of Beacon Hill to a signpost, which marks our way to the left, up the breast of East Harting Down. As the summit of this down is attained, the village of South Harting is seen in the valley, its green church spire making it easily recognisable. West and East Harting are also seen, but these are lesser places. Ahead, in the distance, Butser Hill displays its large and characteristic but unlovable radio mast, and to its right rises Old Winchester Hill.

The track across the down leads to the north of a surfaced car park and a picnic site and just beyond is the B2141, climbing steeply from South Harting.

South Harting is a largish village with a number of timber-framed and eighteenth-century houses. The church, with its green spire contrasting with the tower hung with red tiles, is Early English in style, with two seventeenth-century effigies of the Caryl family, one of whom entertained Alexander Pope at his house Ladyholt. Anthony Trollope lived for a time at South Harting.

We cross the B2141 into a track through a wood, and, following this for a short distance, come to another road, the B2146.

In the triangle between the two roads is Uppark, with the house, which belongs to the National Trust, reached by the B2146, only 1½ kilometres south of the Way. A delightful house and well worth the detour, it was built about 1690 and retains its eighteenth-century furniture and pictures intact — a rare survival. It was offered to Wellington by a grateful government, but when the duke saw the hill from South Harting he declined the offer, saying that he would have been put to the expense of new horses every eighteen months.

In the north of the park, on Tower Hill above the South Downs Way, is a square ruined tower, an eighteenth-century folly, which is visible from various parts of the Way.

We cross the B2146 into Forty Acre Lane, a lane at first wide, but narrowing and becoming rougher. (There is space to park at the beginning of the lane.) It runs at a fairly constant level for about 4

Uppark (north front)

kilometres to the Sussex-Hampshire county boundary, which is the official end of the South Downs Way. Just beyond the unmarked boundary the Way meets a surfaced road, which descends to the South Harting-Petersfield road.

Buses run from South Harting to Petersfield

Few people, I believe, will want to end the Way so indecisively. It may easily be continued to Buriton. Where the Way meets the surfaced road turn left to pass Sunwood Farm. From the farm we follow the road forwards and fork right to go through Cockshot Wood to a sharp left-hand bend a few metres beyond the entrances to Forestry Commission woodland. On the right-hand side of the bend a cart track is signed to Buriton. This descends through the wood, passing under electricity lines, until a sharp right-hand bend beside a small pool. On the left a stile leads to a large field divided by barbed wire fences crossed by a series of stiles. The last stile leads to a lane that turns beside the tree-shaded village pond of Buriton. The church stands beside the pond.

Riders may continue along the cart track, which becomes deeply rutted and muddy, until it meets a surfaced track known as Pitcroft Lane. A left turn and another left turn at the nearby unclassified road brings us to Buriton. Alternatively, continue past the cart track signed to Buriton, a left-hand bend, then one to the right, to Coulters Dean Farm. The surfaced road ends here and beyond is a rutted chalk lane which leads to the Finchdean-Buriton road, which drops down to Buriton by the Maple Inn.

There are occasional buses from the Maple Inn; no service on Sundays. A better service will be found 1½ kilometres north west at Butser crossroads, on the A3.

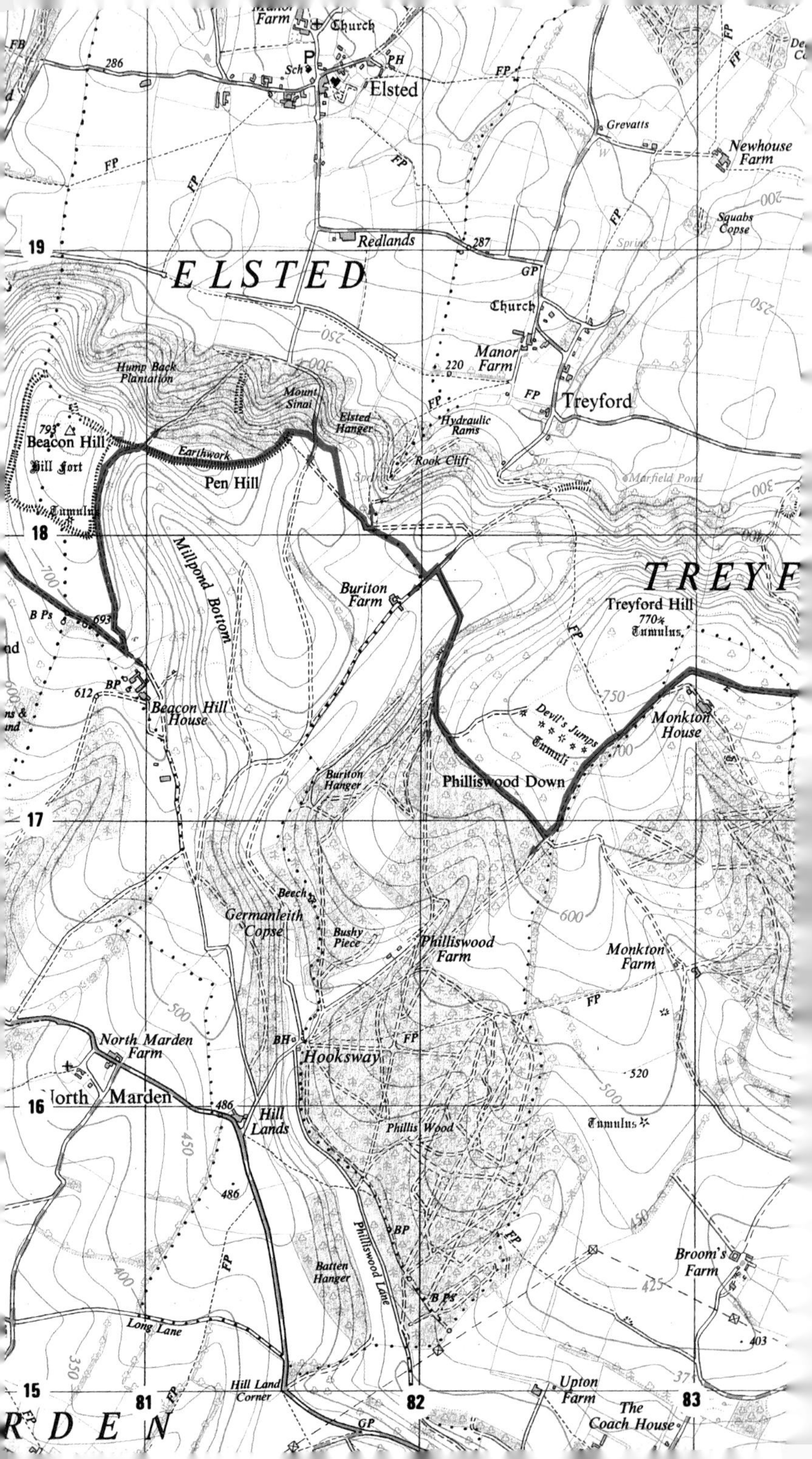
Manor Farm
Church
Sch
PH
Elsted
286
FP
Grevatts
Newhouse Farm
Squabs Copse
Redlands
287
GP
19
ELSTED
Church
Manor Farm
220
Treyford
Hydraulic Rams
Rook Cliff
Marfield Pond
Hump Back Plantation
Mount Sinai
Elsted Hanger
Beacon Hill
Hill Fort
Tumulus
Earthwork
Pen Hill
18
Millpond Bottom
Buriton Farm
TREYF
Treyford Hill
Tumulus
B Ps
693
BP
612
Beacon Hill House
Devil's Jumps
Tumuli
Monkton House
Buriton Hanger
Philliswood Down
17
Beech
Germanleith Copse
Bushy Piece
Philliswood Farm
Monkton Farm
North Marden Farm
BH
Hookway
520
16
North Marden
486
Hill Lands
Phillis Wood
Tumulus
BP
Batten Hanger
Philliswood Lane
Broom's Farm
B Ps
Long Lane
403
15
81
Hill Land Corner
82
Upton Farm
The Coach House
83
GP
R D E N

Pipers Farm
Clay Lane
FP
New Barn
Tile Barn
118
Grevatts Copse
Apsley Copse
150
200
B E P T O N
Park House
Linch Farm
Church Farm
285
Bepton
The Grange
FB
Bugshill Lane
270
295
300
GP
Rectory
288
Didling Hanger
Ash
400
Thorn
Beech
Linch Ball
813
Linch Down
Bepton Down
Rifle Range
Stead Combe
Tumuli
Newfarm Plantn
Tumulus
Cocking Down
Linchball Wood
Bepton Wood
Warren Bottom
Cocking Warren
712
700
Stubbs Copse
Venus Wood
Oak Combe
Hacking Copse
Westdean Woods
Keeper's Cottage
Long Copse
Stapleash Farm
Rabbit Warren
Colworth Down
Colworth Barn
19
18
17
16
15
84
85
86
16

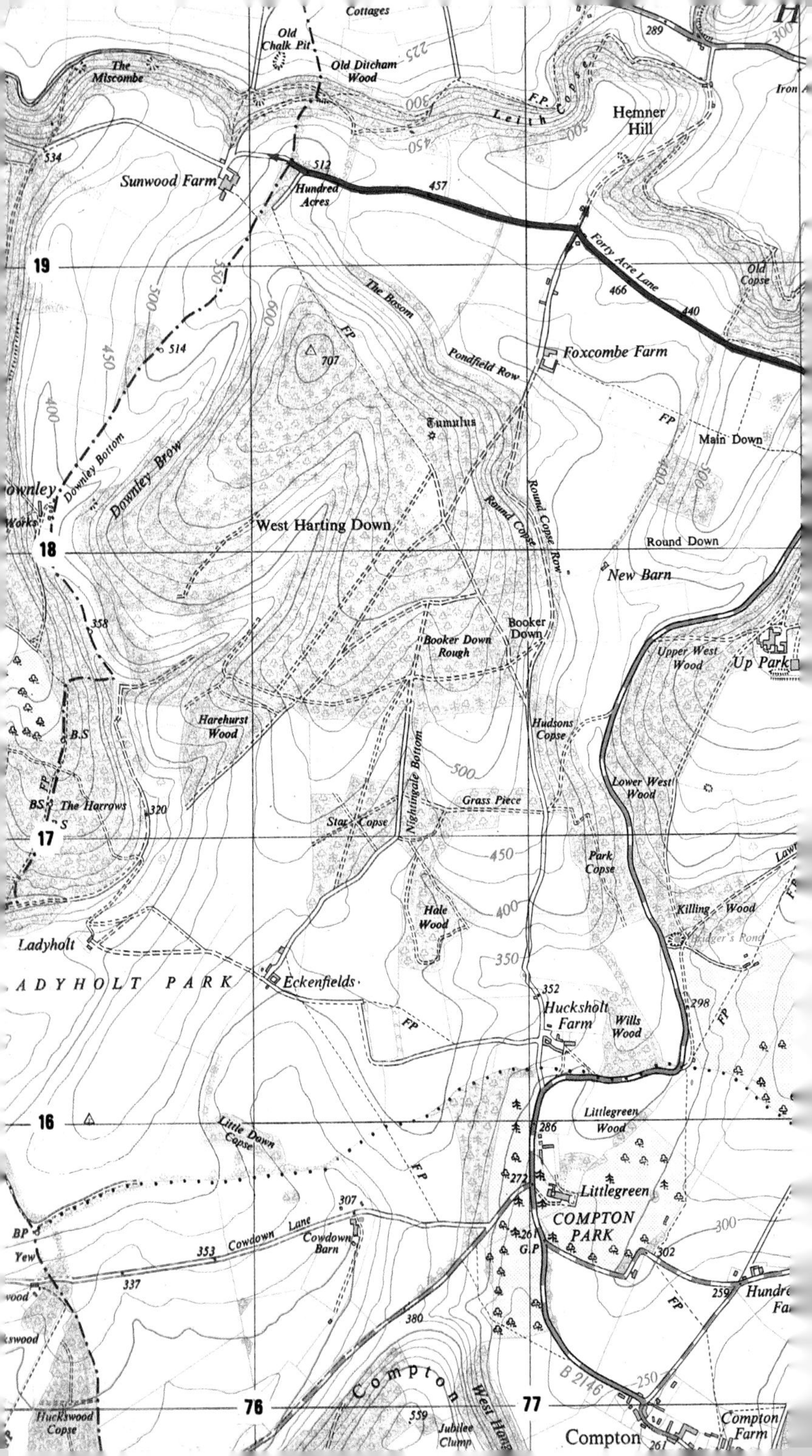
Cottages
Old Chalk Pit
Old Ditcham Wood
The Miscombe
Leith Copse
Hemner Hill
289
534
Sunwood Farm
512
Hundred Acres
457
Forty Acre Lane
Old Copse
466
440
19
The Bosom
514
707
Pondfield Row
Foxcombe Farm
Tumulus
Main Down
Downley Bottom
Downley Brow
Downley
Works
West Harting Down
Round Copse
Round Copse Row
Round Down
18
New Barn
358
Booker Down
Booker Down Rough
Upper West Wood
Up Park
Harehurst Wood
Hudsons Copse
Nightingale Bottom
B.S
Lower West Wood
Grass Piece
The Harrows
320
Star Copse
17
Park Copse
Killing Wood
Hale Wood
Ladyholt
ADYHOLT PARK
Eckenfields
352
Hucksholt Farm
Wills Wood
298
16
Littlegreen Wood
Little Down Copse
286
272
Littlegreen
307
COMPTON PARK
Cowdown Lane
Cowdown Barn
353
261
302
259
337
380
B 2146
Compton
76
77
559
Jubilee Clump
Huckswood Copse
Compton Farm
FP

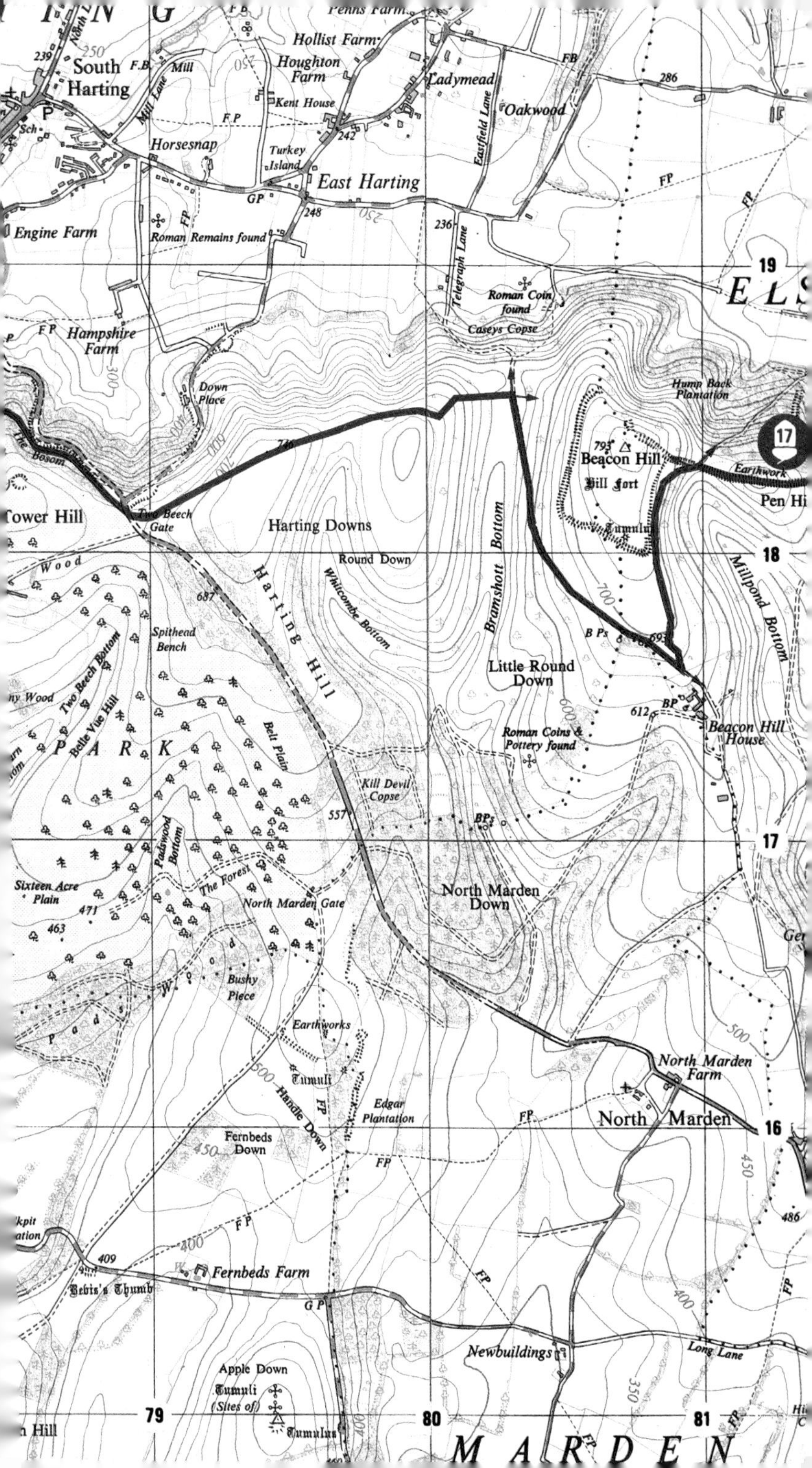

South Harting
Sch
Mill Lane
Mill
F.B
Hollist Farm
Houghton Farm
Kent House
Penns Farm
Ladymead
Oakwood
Eastfield Lane
FB
286
F P
Horsesnap
Turkey Island
242
East Harting
GP
248
250
236
Telegraph Lane
FP
Engine Farm
Roman Remains found
19
E L S
Roman Coin found
Caseys Copse
Hampshire Farm
300
Down Place
Hump Back Plantation
17
746
793
Beacon Hill
Hill Fort
Earthwork
Tumulus
Pen Hi
The Bosom
Tower Hill
Two Beech Gate
Harting Downs
Bramshott Bottom
18
Wood
Round Down
Millpond Bottom
687
Harting Hill
Whitcombe Bottom
700
Spithead Bench
B Ps
693
Little Round Down
Two Beech Bottom
Belle Vue Hill
P A R K
Belt Plain
612
BP
Beacon Hill House
Roman Coins & Pottery found
Kill Devil Copse
557
BPs
Padswood Bottom
Sixteen Acre Plain
471
463
The Forest
North Marden Gate
North Marden Down
Bushy Piece
Earthworks
500
Tumuli
Handle Down
Edgar Plantation
North Marden Farm
North Marden
16
Fernbeds Down
450
FP
486
400
409
Fernbeds Farm
Bevis's Thumb
G P
Newbuildings
Long Lane
350
Apple Down
Tumuli (Sites of)
Tumulus
79
80
81
M A R D E N

Places of interest by the Way

Arundel

As seen from the valley where the main road runs, the town of Arundel is splendidly picturesque, climbing a hill to its two great buildings, the Catholic cathedral of St Philip Neri and the great Norman fortress of the Dukes of Norfolk. The town is, however, very small. The cathedral, built by the 15th earl and completed in 1876, is in French Gothic style, and its soaring design is emphasised by the hill on which it stands. The parish church of St Nicholas is modest by comparison; it dates from the fourteenth century. The chancel forms the Fitzalan chapel — the Fitzalans held the castle for three hundred years up to 1580 — and it contains monuments of the Fitzalan Earls of Arundel and of their successors the Howard Dukes of Norfolk; the latter have through many generations been Earls Marshal of England. The Honour of Arundel was granted by the Conqueror to Roger de Montgomery, who built the castle. The fortress was besieged in 1102 and in 1139, and again in 1643–4 by the Cromwellian Waller, who battered large parts of the building into ruins. It was rebuilt in the eighteenth century in Regency Gothic, and rebuilt again in more scholarly style late in the nineteenth century. The castle stands in a huge park extending 3 kilometres northwards towards the South Downs Way. Castle and park are open to visitors.

Brighton

The largest of the seaside resorts of Sussex, spreading far along the coast and inland over the downs and joining in an extensive conurbation with Hove, Portslade, Southwick, and Shoreham. Beginning as a fishing village called Brighthelmstone, it began to expand after Dr. Richard Russell established a curative centre about 1754; he recommended sea-bathing and the drinking of sea water. The place was made fashionable by George IV, who, as Prince of Wales, lived here in a house designed by Henry Holland. Over the following forty years this house was transformed in the Chinese and then in the Indian taste into the fantastic and marvellous Royal Pavilion, which is now owned by the Corporation and contains much of the furniture of its heyday. With all the attractions of a seaside resort, much elegant architecture, and its famous Lanes full of antique treasure trove, Brighton keeps abreast of modern trends with shopping precincts, a conference and entertainment centre, multi-storey and underground car parks, and Europe's largest marina. On the outskirts is the University of Sussex, with interesting buildings in a modern idiom, next to one of Brighton's most picturesque parks, Stanmer, once the estate of the Earls of Chichester.

Chichester

The cathedral city of Sussex and a town of great antiquity, probably the tribal capital of the Regni, whose leader Cogidubnus was a client king to the Romans. It retains many remnants and buildings of its long history, notably the great Norman cathedral, which was built about 1070. The spire, rebuilt in the nineteenth century, is said to be the only English cathedral spire visible from the sea; it is also visible from the South Downs Way. In the centre of the town is the Butter Cross, built about 1500. There are many other medieval and later buildings of monastic or ecclesiastical origin, and in the area known as the Pallants some handsome eighteenth-century houses. Historically and aesthetically, Chichester is a town of considerable interest.

Eastbourne

A large seaside resort, which began to develop in the 1860s, and has spread inland to surround the old town of East Bourne. The new town was a monument to the Duke of Devonshire, who owned the land and controlled the manner in which the resort developed. Eastbourne still reflects its origin in a character distinct from that of other resorts. Something of the old town survives round the medieval church of St Mary, whose structure is largely twelfth-century. Behind it is the Old Parsonage House, built of flint in the early sixteenth century, and in the churchyard are the remains of ancient crosses. The situation of Eastbourne, where the long beach ends at the chalk cliffs of Beachy Head, is felicitous, as walkers on the South Downs Way will agree.

Goodwood

Goodwood House, set on the southern slopes of the downs near Chichester, has been the seat of the Dukes of Richmond since 1720. Built to an unusual three-sided plan, it contains beautiful furniture and fine pictures, and stands in an extensive wooded park. It is open to the public and on certain days visits are combined with lunch or tea. North of the house is Goodwood race course, where race meetings are held, notably in July. St Roche's Hill, or 'the Trundle', has wide-spreading views.

Glynde

The picturesque village stands next to a good Elizabethan mansion built of stone and flint, which has the distinction, with the previous house on the site, of never having been sold over a period of seven hundred years — it has passed from branch to branch of the same family. It stands in pleasant gardens. One of the owners, Bishop Richard Trevor, Bishop of Durham, built the church in 1765, in a good classical style.

Glyndebourne, to the south, is famous the world over for its operatic performances.

Lancing

Lancing's church of St James is of Norman foundation, altered in the fourteenth century. It is far outdone in splendour by the huge chapel of Lancing College, which soars above the valley of the Adur north of the A27 — it is visible from the South Downs Way. The chapel, in the French Gothic style of the thirteenth century, was begun in 1868. The founder of the college and the chapel was Canon N. Woodward, who intended a series of English public schools and did in fact found a number of them — in Sussex at Hurstpierpoint and at Ardingly. Lancing College chapel, a noble building by R. H. Carpenter, contains fine modern tapestries. It is open to visitors.

Lewes

The county town of East Sussex, takes its name from a Saxon word *hlaew,* meaning a hill. It is strategically placed at the foot of Cliffe Hill and the Caburn, where the Ouse makes a gap in the Downs, and William de Warenne, to whom the Conqueror had given the rape of Lewes, built a great castle here. Its remains may be seen, as may also the ruins of the Cluniac priory (near the station) founded by Warenne and his wife Gundrada. Her grave slab is in the church of St. John the Baptist. Several remaining medieval churches testify to the importance of the town that grew up in the shelter of the castle. It was walled in the fourteenth century. In the Marian persecutions of the sixteenth century fourteen persons were burnt in the Market Place; a monument on Cliffe Hill commemorates them. The Gunpowder Plot inspired extraordinary festivities, which are continued every year with great celebration. The eighteenth century was a time of prosperity in Lewes, when many new buildings were erected and old ones refaced (but many timber-framed buildings remain). It gave Lewes a character it has retained to this day. There are two excellent museums of the Sussex Archaeological Society, in Barbican House and in Anne of Cleves' House, the latter a sixteenth-century building once owned by the divorced wife of Henry VIII. In the Battle of Lewes in 1264 Henry III was defeated by the barons' party led by Simon de Montfort.

Parham House

A restored Elizabethan house set in a splendid park at the foot of the downs below Rackham Hill. It is open to the public. It contains fine Elizabethan, Jacobean, and Georgian portraits together with furniture of these periods and needlework. South of the house is the small medieval church of St James, remaining from a village that once stood here. It contains a leaden font of 1351. In the park are deer and a notable heronry.

The Weald

The Weald is all the country between the North Downs and the South Downs, extending in the east into Kent and in the west into Hampshire. Its name means woodland, and for centuries the Weald was densely wooded and difficult of access. As seen from the Downs it still appears thickly wooded, but many of the ancient woods were felled by iron-founders and ship-builders.

Weald and Downland Open-Air Museum, Singleton

The idea of an open-air museum was formed in 1965 and two years later the present beautiful site of sloping fields and woodlands was obtained. Here have been rebuilt several interesting and remarkable buildings that faced destruction in their original situations. These buildings are nearly all timber-framed. They included barns and cattle-sheds, a small building containing a treadwheel over a well, granaries (one of which was brought in one piece from Goodwood), a market hall, small cottages, a water-mill, and a lovely jettied Wealden farmhouse. All these have been reconstructed as they originally were, and they serve to give the visitor an idea how the people of former times lived. Plans for additional buildings are well advanced. There are also exhibits showing how country industries such as carpentry, charcoal-burning, and pottery were carried on. Visitors may picnic on the site.

Restored Elizabethan Parham House

The Country Code

Enjoy the countryside and respect its life and work

Guard against all risk of fire

Fasten all gates

Keep your dogs under close control

Keep to public paths across farmland

Use gates and stiles to cross fences, hedges and walls

Leave livestock, crops and machinery alone

Take your litter home

Help to keep all water clean

Protect wildlife, plants and trees

Take special care on country roads

Make no unnecessary noise

Looking east from Ditchling Beacon

Further reading and reference

Along the South Downs Way, David Harrison. Cassell, London, 1958.
On Foot in Sussex, A. A. Evans. 1933.
Sussex, John Burke. Batsford, London, 1974.
The Sussex Landscape, Peter Brandon. Hodder & Stoughton, London, 1974.
Sussex (Little Guides series), Ronald F. Jessup. Methuen, London, 1957.
Sussex (Buildings of Britain series), Ian Nairn and Nikolaus Pevsner. Penguin Books, London, 1965.
The Wealden District (British Regional Geology series), R. W. Gallois. H.M.S.O., 1968.
Geology and Scenery in England and Wales, A. E. Trueman, Penguin Books, London, 1963.
Geological Survey Ten-Mile Map sheet 2, Ordnance Survey, 1957.
Flora of Sussex, A. H. Wolley-Dodd. Kenneth Saville, Hastings, 1937.
Wild Flowers of the Chalk and Limestone (New Naturalists series), J. E. Lousley. Collins, London, 1950.
The Shell Natural History of Britain, ed. Maurice Burton. Michael Joseph, London, 1970.
Prehistoric England, Grahame Clark. Batsford, London, 1962.
Prehistoric Britain, Jacquetta and Christopher Hawkes. Penguin Books, London, 1963.
The Concise Oxford Dictionary of English Place-Names, Eilert Ekwall. Oxford University Press, 4th ed., 1960.
Walks along the South Downs Way, Lord Charles Teviot. Spurbooks Ltd., 1973.
Chalkways of South and South-East England, Edward C. Pyatt. David & Charles, Newton Abbot, 1974.
Twenty Walks West of Arun, Charles Shippam. Phillimore & Co., 1973.
Along the South Downs Way. Eastbourne Rambling Club. (Includes accommodation list.)
Bed and Breakfast Guide. Ramblers' Association. Annual.
Camping Sites of Great Britain. Link House. Annual.
Campsites in Britain. Lett's. Annual.
Where to Stay in South-East England. English Tourist Board. Annual.